Ambrosia of the Netherworld

Ambrosia of the Netherworld

H. D. Moe
With an introduction by Jack Foley

TAUREAN HORN PRESS
Petaluma, California

ISBN 10: 0-931552-19-2
ISBN 13: 978-0-931552-19-9
Library of Congress Control Number: 2023933765

Cover Painting by Jim Scott, "Still Life with Onions."

Photographs of H. D. Moe by Steve Wilson

Printed in The U.S.A.
TAUREAN HORN PRESS
P.O. Box 526
Petaluma, CA 94953

INTRODUCTION

by Jack Foley

The force of the seizure woke him. It shattered his will and tore at his insides. It destroyed the capacity of his soul to waver, as it often had in youth without intending, between the multitude of worlds.

■

Something impossible was happening and he sat helpless in its full assault.

—Jake Berry, *Brambu Drezi,* Book III

Ambrosia: "In the ancient Greek myths, ambrosia (Greek: ἀμβροσία, "[h]aom[a]-sustenance") is sometimes the food or drink of the Greek gods, often depicted as conferring longevity or immortality upon whoever consumed it" (Wikipedia).

What is "Ambrosia of the *Nether*world" — Ambrosia of Hell or Hades, the "lower" world? The late H.D. Moe's book begins,

Just past staggering bambi metaphysics
climbing out into quick unreal daylight
time/space fold over space/time
beany-cap electric rubber-band
hummingbird mediating upon a phone-line
distance takes off up-close
feeling carefully narrows subtlety
holding grail-cup eardrums via pinky
after the index
universal necessity karmas
breathing steam-rooms
hiccupping clocks across the west
chasing instantaneous twang

eyebrows vibra-harp
sinews of iterated dreams

Many of Moe's poems are comic in their bizarre juxtapositions—
and intentionally so. I remember his low chuckles as he read
them, his amused delight in his own fabrications. Consider a
passage like this:

let's switcharoo our dwellings to longevity communes
let's turn our prisons into imagination-transforming universities
& spring padded zoos
WHAT'S WRONG WITH THE NUTTEHUMPYO
GRAND CANYON EARS
nuttiehumpyu
nuttee   nuttehumpyo
nuttiehumpyee
nuttium
nute humpyu
nuttehumpyu   noteehumpo
notee
nutteehumpoem
not
nutahsumbe
nuttehumpyo
nutteehump
nootoo bump po

which Moe read and pronounced a little differently every time
he read it.

The opening of *Ambrosia of the Netherworld* is different from
that. Moe (1937-2013) knew he was dying when he wrote this
book and knew as well that the book would be published after
his death. The words here sound like a man talking fast—saying
anything that pops into his head in an effort to stave off his all-
too-imminent eternal silence. As long as he can talk (write), he
is alive: "sinews of iterated dreams."

And yet, the talk *is* "ambrosial," a delight—even in the face of the "netherworld." And wasn't it that archetype of the poet, Orpheus, who descended into the netherworld and charmed everyone and everything? And came out alive, albeit having lost his beloved? Is Moe Orpheus here? Are we all his Eurydices?

Not quite. *Ambrosia of the Netherworld* is no allegory of death and rebirth: H.D. Moe was far too cheerful and life-loving for that to be the case. Lines like these abound:

> *die-well lifts his sword from the gravy-train*
> *rises like totem waters metamorphed into a second jib*
> *ding-a-ling between my nose for unseen ubiquity*
> *rages in a storm of wild cellos*

Yet the book has the whiff of the knowledge of death about it, and that knowledge colors everything. *Ambrosia of the Netherworld* is, as Moe puts it, *"hip to skidoo"*:

kindling fireflies to light the mother-fucking universe
estoria at nesqwin, gulls forlorn withering television-sets coming in-from beatrice
lost elementary-school ancient children just reincarnated form old souls new drive-in

It is wonderful to encounter the patented madness of this poet of dreams and language and to feel that, just maybe, language can bring him back. "Books," wrote Milton in the *Areopagitica,* "are not absolutely dead things, but do contain a potency of life in them to be as active as that soul was whose progeny they are; nay, they do preserve as in a vial the purest efficacy and extraction of that living intellect that bred them...a good book is the precious lifeblood of a master spirit, embalmed and treasured up on purpose to a life beyond life." Milton was not wrong about that. H.D. Moe is here in all the aliveness of his mastery—a kind of transcendent dyslexia (or in Moe's phrase, "dyslexic portmanteau"):

yes, I'm a born utopian
shebanging the whole-thing in the open

No one would accuse this clown prince of writing like his old friend, Jake Berry, whose great *Brambu Drezi* is in part a hymn to oblivion, to the perception of death-in-life: "I came here to speak of the gathering dead / in the smell of singed hair." Yet Moe is like Berry in his deep perception of "the multitude of worlds" and of their vast collision. Like Berry, Moe perceives that "Something impossible [is] happening," and like Berry he sits "helpless in its full assault." The Impossible was H.D. Moe's daily bread and—impossibly—here he is again, microphoning us from an underground that feels undeniably like life:

Falling through holy wisdom
numbskull jellyfish
voodoo leatherworks
bugged memes
katmandu gumdrops
multi-vitaminizing nightmares' round-up
freyja drawn by wild purity
revelation carried away within the dark

"Alone in our vastness." Note how often that word "alone" shows up in this book!

—JACK FOLEY
October, 2015

Ambrosia of the
Netherworld

Just past staggering bambi metaphysics
climbing out into quick unreal daylight
time/space fold over space/time
beany-cap electric rubber-band
hummingbird mediating upon a phone-line
distance takes off up-close
feeling carefully narrows subtlety
holding grail-cup eardrums via pinky
after the index
universal necessity karmas
breathing steam-rooms
hiccupping clocks across the west
chasing instantaneous twang
eyebrows vibra-harp
sinews of iterated dreams
intellectual workers
metaphoring theories
inversely proportionate
to all dimension
liberty escaping itself
open like an immortal stem-cell
template of every form of life
whims in the memory of phantoms
unidentified shade give-a-ways
re-arrested for impersonating your archetype
weeping jungian mousgateers
feeling touch-up
downpour hardwarestores
de pak chopra unpacking reformation
living injun nearly
ecology our church
teeth lightening-bolt
slow banana dawn
arising to flourish you

I-ching write ouija plots riddled tick-tock yugas
fabulous immortal medicine invented by a non-regressive

hypnotist
who decides to ensconce ghostwriting the apocalypse
    dimension?
with the formula of eternity, quantum paths bare-feet upon a
    country-road
hitting metal starry window driving nowhere
into raindrops washing away the southern bugs
die-well lifts his sword from the gravy-train
rises like totem waters metamorphed into a second jib
ding-a-ling between my nose for unseen ubiquity
rages in a storm of wild cellos
kindling fireflies to light the mother-fucking universe
estoria at nesqwin, gulls forlorn withering television-sets
    coming in-from beatrice
lost elementary-school ancient children just reincarnated form
    old souls new drive-in
zipping thru duration quick-fasts anything other than titles no-
    time
headstrong omer kiam chased irish-bagpipe stomach
quite enough reading about brainy membrane theories
startled kosmos avatar under the shade of this olive tree
open your echo

Spontaneous inhibition glinting cobweb networks
haptic impulse knit precluding always judgment
thanatopsis forever birth weaving rues
meandering visionary landscapes
with my inspired-lady hip to skidoo
diaphanous cats-cradle
taffy-pull upon a loom
evolutionary vortex
trumpet or venus-flytrap?
memes dna
sailing in & out the cellar
hermes junket ganymede
bio-friendly universe
reaching homestretch

string-'em-up guitar
high on wit's twang
are ideologies pillars of non-residence?
being lost reveals itself in a dream so we may awake
between sciences' drunken proof
& goofy nerve-cells' organizing anarchist
zugzwang pawnbroker dueling over-the-fence

My sky appears
breaking-out into a ganglia parachute
faith our initiate numinous realm quiet
enflamed, launching madam blavatsky's cucumber
where ye kowtow nods all extremists become madcap
devil's punch-bowl eyes blazing thailand's orange-heaven
light this up in neon pulse kinetic gestalt.
are you hung-up on what just passed ahead?
switch-a-roo thru your dizziness
 if & only if never before
you saw universals' atomic eden
depart upon the plains
like a camel in the honey wind
as inside tent-shows balloon space to infinite whims
elaborate lethe swimming into nothing's bliss
ice-cream time-cones raking ache
on a heroin seahorse
nowhere yes, I'm a born utopian
shebanging the whole-thing in the open

Falling through holy wisdom
numbskull jellyfish
voodoo leatherworks
bugged memes
katmandu gumdrops
multi-vitaminizing nightmares' round-up
freyja drawn by wild purity
revelation carried away within the dark

no overseer, understanding between
just fly quicker than your shadow
as enrapture wraps its velvet throw
pronounce here nervous roars around
drumming tattoos invisibly kenspeckled with guru shrouds
buried in libraries, guillotined by isagoge pagination
swallowtail mindfulness jink into this weightless light
unqualified, naked, I'm empty like an onion, fencing tears
yet there's no resting anything to stop to name
no immovable type or mathematics of white
adapting kinetic ethers, orphic big-bang shibboleths
tractable unknowns building golem's eraser
revising dreams bring me fugued asleep
swims inundating virtual neutrality
thru jet-black the unique of is
reeling backward the glossary of timing dynamite hellos
awakened huff 'n puffs whisper intimate come-heres
rising alive beyond the swamp of death
oh feel ya knuckling dew from her lashes
illapsing in on a rose-parade-float
cradling grins, signaling us, hearts,
mickeymousing out of thy dash
wiggle-room politics crazy acid enigmas
odder than the never-happened
immediacy visits our loony-bin
aluminum-foil decks the next-door's bedpost
reflective defense against lip-synch wounds' cry
elite underlings, lazy sensitives, the mendacity of victim-hood
where toothy beehives yardbird kilroys to skinheads on a jew's
    harp
inner & outer-space with clear empty in-between, laughing
    tavern mouths
igloo pompadours, aliens human, threading dolphins,
    windows of the skin
smeared by mirrors' here & gone lucidity, fins quicker than
    quantum collapse
infinite-layered highways whispering leads to gibraltar's brain-
    drain

immunology remote, jibing incognito, unidentified by modal
quizzes
acassic founder, virgil, beany-capped up like a pregnant teeter-
totter
alighting onto histories' gun-running-crouch
indian ear haunting radio-shack of cheerful knives
smithereening meanders, humpty-dumpty in a nutshell,
exposed via the tip-off pine-tree universe, reaching
meaningful chow-downs, giving lullabies of shakespeare
where-not-to-go dostovesky absurdly hibernating the
firmament decomposing yahvas, radiating elemental
pioneers' intimate mind, touching warm glass, always
outside, forever in

Ecology god
both multiple & at one
undivided in potential
completely free, exploring with sunlight hands
raying over wigs of misunderstanding
powdered by birth dust
ground into alchemies
teleological yearning
on mad legs spidering across abysses
weaving a network, orgasms & galaxies
puffed-up sand-dunes castling into rene descartes
mathematical fate juggernauting upon hopeful turn-arounds
cart-wheeling sans origin to no end
appointments wide-open
receptive distillations gauntleting jibes
feeling the path laying down before within me
guided by infinite reins & super-string puppeteers
lines idle-wildly trailing chaos' nutmeg
heaps of dawn whittling beaver-dams
tautologically snowing atop of everything
violining fire under rational checkpoint kick-offs
dubbing nameless, aiming sum-ups
rebelling liberty each moment

breathing knives, whistling tears
spinning leonardo di vinci again
humankind's electron roulette makes flight
'twixt an is that isn't, quickly bare-footing prints
'neath thunder across kisses' surf
immediately unique may you forever appear

Vibe currents under my wing-ding bellhop
doing the egyptain up the hitchcock stairs
lighthouses to the nooisphere
orwellian wishingwells
in the rabbit-holes of teli vev
crisscross galaxies' sky
just looking for this dimension
felt occasions wheeling off
upon velvet roads
blues in the over-studied park
zoo-books switch-a-rooed
its gravy-train released
everyone at once jumping-jupiter
I'm flying with haunted pageboys
chicken-littles roller-skating mels-drive-in
elves or brainy-kids water-falling rainbows
diana leaps upon me from thy hidden cliff
mahogany twilight suffuses my zeus
& under the beginning of eve
genius has a limit.

Razorblade winking from spinoza's mirror
hegeling eeore lean-too to wigwam
infinitely counting down the acassic-bank
who's tobogganing our essential lines anyway?
kindling bo-did-a-lee? dharma skitzode?
pussyfooting up to her lion eyes
torch-run thru jekel & hyde
grounded by unknown energy
mother-load, bad-ass, aunt jemmyma

beyond remote dweeps
winkum-blinkum on-the-quad
nul-odds to summon bonum
communist in alien selfhood's nom de plume
festooning a neutral entry thru impenetrable chaos
in-between my overhead
underground, backpacking the above

Jumping leaps, flesh broken open in a weeping quarry, diving
    cheers
snowflakes twinkle in one's hair from our shared prison of
    limited existence
clear mirrors without reflection breathe like invisible windows
    thru holiness
we don't ken as we galumph along behind these mirages of
    hallucinatory survival
desperately outsourcing, gold fever insanity clawing into
    libraries for dawns' escape-hatch
since night as will said where no dreams may come,
    approaches & is here, just draw in your jowls & peer into
    your moony skull flashing reincarnated mistakes bathed in
    amniotic darkrooms rising memories of who you actually
    never were or will be
listen now sans all goalposts to the music of trees, each one,
    each needle, branch, leaf
configuring with the breeze a unique symphony, lifting minds
    to immortal endeavors
helpful robots personalized to each you-who, alchemies of
    gastronomical stardust
fugued levels' estranged beginnings never ahead, unknown,
    invented huddles
exploding grab-bag out of zilch containing all that is now,
    falling toward inertia
paralyzed by dream, kinetic reveries swinging on the waves,
    inundating edgewise
cued along drunken thoroughfares, quick fixes, masks upon
    shields veiled with an honesty

incompletely purloined mystic goo accelerated in every
    slowdown, isness, bondage
abyss full of other-than, vacuuming ubiquity weathervanes, a
    pebble sailing from the hip.

Well, dingbat let's emulge about
swing in kung fu aesthetics, learning baby-talk
dawning computer's private guide, orphic virgil
misspelled by the unknown
admiral you gybeing around this island of festoons
within a volcano, nodding past yesterdays' caveman
diving jackknives to the swan, I'm embrangle as one dark tent
    while
contra-intuitive modal universes x-ray our yardbird minds
like winking ping-pong buffer-zones of the white goddess
scrying ovary's eureka raindrop
lip-syncing calypso zoot-suiting auras haloing thru durations
    of time-bias
wolfshit vibes towheaded in-between the mistletoe, roaring
    unions' creation
lawless empathy, when individual jiving phone-booths wakeup
    to fabulous truth
then comes oscar wilde with a dick broken off on your last
    statue
love-tunes, airways, bebop hippopotamus sidewalks tweet
    cloudbank
tobogganing innings sans end, gurdjieff, donald-duck & lillian
    gish
happy as the 3 musketeers trying to fly a chocolate teeter-
    totter
clad in black petals of ezra pound, foraging the mohave
rock-climbing alive snapping-turtle think-tanks, crazy-glue
    websites
engraved stones hair-waving dromedaries from a golden ring-
    a-ling
angeling over what's real, yet not exactly light-bulbed in netflix
remote castling kneecaps articulated portals' other everland

reversing gravity, shift hiatus, implanted, breakout of jungian
funhouses
swimming the moment like amnesia's placebo, could be
everywhere
listening hearsay, gemini wheeling mark twain, swarthy
nightfall tip your ace
razor sleeping upside-down, olfactory elbows kicking chubby-
checker breathe
gyroing now orient yarns relational taffy-pull stick to your
muscling-guns
there's unguilty sinews puppeting you, names outrunning city-
blocks
wizard tombs meditating, breathing glasses enfolded in an
insect pose
antennae dousing taps, startling hidden valentines, bleeding
redwoods
william shakespeare female mosquitoes quietly alight,
engineering
hot fudge knighthood, just ahead of laughing gas chambers'
tautology errand boy
quantum mongoose ubiquity powwow smithereens up against
rattles
hickory-dickory-docking everybodies'gong-show when my
baby-guru reassures dawn
smiling coastline's terrific pacific rollypolly kettledrums zither
nervous seesaw limbo across india's teleological horizon
fiddlesticks jackdaw shell-shocked nest-egg reverberating to
mercury's birth gaugan tiptoes overture albinos
pussyfoots upon lily-livered enlightenment humming tiny fly-
apart's doorbell
nipples ufoing for the utopian g-spot
lumpen-proletariat, highbrow in on celestial ski jumps
act, invent zilch, glow-worm paths earthen dust
commingling with milky-way jisom, landing blossoms' nut-job
rocketing inhibition, slow-down into yuga pendulums eardrum
mandala
open clickity-clack jabberwalky-talky boxcars empty of all
thought

feeling quick wisdom..

Whorling away from centering shiboliths
obliterating every membrane of individual birthing
without living vivarium & context, raging tears
smash thru us like numb bullets, knives
sharking our care, our frames of togetherness
ice picking the brain in little incessant stabs
lightening-bolts terroring across my chest
vacuums of nausea empty of all but pain
flooding my whole being until I'm nothing
except a cry for death howling to this dumb random succubus
splintering everything I am, was & may be, mind, emotion,
    body
to cutting mirrors of non-remembrance, diamond teeth with
    no feeling roots
breaking down & dissolving each portal & doorway of
    understanding, consuming unto total chaotic void finally
    itself even, indifferent icebergs ripping apart all entity's
    integrity, emerging now around, within, between you & I ,
    replete, throughout, non-stoppable by anything my living
    knows, out of any guidance whatsoever, impersonal childish
    fugue-state with nada boundaries, an omnivorous black hole
    sans intelligence sans exit is gobbling down to this voice,
    I'm screaming to you, engulfed by raging, weeping flames
    of a hell beyond measure, gulping in bottomless gulps, who
    we are & ever will be.

Sidesaddle, ideas of glee
trot by petticoated over with shrouds of light
enough to mistake any import for lovely death's authority
misspent economical ideas like dumb-dumb bullets hollow as
    empty zen, arch to descend
again at my foot before my undefeated dance is hurt via their
    thin firmament
ideas are plunging into birth's lower dark like whales &
    shovels, grave-digging sing-a-longs

gathering & drawing together via the pied-piping of illusional
   freedom, mineral spirits holding up
deems hypnotizing yird's elements to arise machinelike
   juggernauting over my gentle wildness
imprisoning me in utopian dinosaurs wheeling all I am in
   this bodily form toward probable demise engineering sans
   intimacy horror vacuuming weapons distancing us from any
   love
we have left, these viral corrupters of feeling, these monadical-
   memes invading life's
dreaming genes, trapped in books & websites they await
   poised on their flea-like hunches
to spring upon this alive novelling continuum we are, to suck
   up our flow into zones, categories
vows & laws, either/or bating debates without union in-
   betweens, over & underdetermining lopsided schematics
   careening extremes, dividing blushes down unto the
   false rose of a politician's ashen cigar, touching off
   internecine antinomies so oceans of expression become
   the government's trickle & anyone-else's dry creek, not as
   important as picabia's skullduggery underwear, discard all
   ideas, be naked inside your now/here feeling enlightenment,
   you know what you yoyo need to know in your benign
   nuttiness, what way to go to bring about the big potential
   uncurling ancient/new wisdom
continually given from the baby-god whose aura laurel of
   mind is unenclosed nor crucified by any idea, our frames
   of natural adaptation have evolved long-ago deeply
   wider than & beyond thoughts clinging onto & making up
   every ideology, deconstruct all ideas, space & roll them
   individually & collectively down to unique skeleton keys
   releasing everyone to butterfly their mind, alighting upon &
   transcending our flowering plantitude, once done, awakened
   beings, you'll have no jail of self to open, no basement of
   heaven to lock, totally unknown & known, jiving the fibs of
   living whys, you'll be accepted by the organic understanding
   that is the is. Oh gypsy sunsets & dawn encamped on
   the coursing nile, fundamental as our intelligence rhymes

with the past, yet never returns as immediate tomorrow's
dido, we loyally wing on, adventuress, experimenters of
whatever's found & made, simultaneously climbing &
descending our intuitional ladders of give & take, fingering
here a wake for idea, let's travel stillness with our thumbs
enfolded in the palms of happy ease, let's unbuild all into
slow growing just infinity
riding on our own hips, freeing at their own pace all we may
from the battling chains of morality, belief & idea, before
they kill us, before we're drawn into the kafka pyramid
of no escape, release me from written rituals, from the taking
of sides closing in on me now, I hear the official whispering
of clouds in my muscles, the falling of drowning sand

Bag-piping all I can stomach
insides held like nosegay trumpets
clear of osmosis even
scrying gestalts within the dangling vineyard universe
cradled by relations threaded via maelstroms
& palimpsests onioning to no ding-en-sich
except a seemly dream free of inertia, rocking banana grins
gathering to this heretofore now that mathematically is
is everlastingly infinite always becoming smithereened
into each grace-note, raying forth typhoons leaning our hair
cyclones pompadoring himalaya's minted emotion, amazing
    labyrinths' jigsaw smoo
winnowing intricate time-warps, baby-fuzz radars,
    underlooking enzymes, fluxing yaweh
correcting intuitions, lifted momentums, dialogs echoing
    timber thru soundless rage
powwowing with hidebound anathemas, dropkicking curtains
    of maddening nightfall
wistful syzygy gliding over dunce-caps & teething buzz-saws
    unto heroin arrowheads
raining on us like inverted vogswagon fortune-cookies,
    emptying wise clichés, occipital lullabies, pictures with
    nothing in them but suck-ups & zero bombardiers' mirror of

wit's last drip, pear-shaped & hanging atop calm tomorrow's
    drum-roll, thundering upon my earth-birth
reverberating incarnations flashing past ancestral scrimshaws,
    dancing childhood on grandpa winks, a swallowtail
    liberty cocooned in imaginal genes between all themes,
    unwrapping rhapsodies' turban wound crying out to you Oh
    yellow heaven awakening, rusted by disappearing synergies,
    vortexing teleology drill-bit's breakthrough, magnifying,
    kindling
hands of cool flames, touchdowning on keystone arpeggios,
    signaling everyone beyond index.

When all political sides reside in our intelligent muscle &
    emotions
like yin-yang boomerangs curling within the game of oneself
fascism decisions acknowledged now to keep urchin majorities
    safe
any belief no longer here encumbering us with its rosy dark
    church lens of disfigurement
its superfluous veneer mummifying alive natural cradling
    experience
then we will be as we are: vertebrates, housing transcendental
    minds
& via the ancient childrening of this & maybe other universes
everyone, from these individual, collective sensoriums, upping
    discovers, inventors
dawning an old/new mythological information ageless brainy
    stagecoach
climb on there's mucho room for all who want to giddy-up
    toward eternity
whoa down & spread-out their horizons of mirror-genes, their
    loving kindness
enfold in waves of our caring gianthood, the repugnant, crazy,
    idiosyncratic, untoward
we're together & akin with, no need for john locke contracts or
    everlasting vows
I now release you from your jails of belief & turn all pens into

23

learning groves of trees
deep rooted in wild adventures & understanding, plumbing
   like yeats with humor & a sword
of discrimination, the kosmos within the psyche's galaxy &
   dust mote.

Alone in our vastness
intimate & distant
speaking pulses
waving here to nowhere
knowing quieter than minds
flying in, worn aware
dangling up-side-down
batty high goodbyes
standouts atop paginated crests
blinding enlightenments
only afterward unseen like it was
opium tar-babies cooking in the pipes of night's return
burning within limbs asleep released
flickering quicker any imagination
is thou beyond you I or it itself
juiced with every other thou sans edge
directing & yet pointless inside the searching always
cradling hells of joy
feeling rules dumbfounded
informing beauty to gesture truth never quite true while
this irish maid jives alive sinbad cinemas full of bob hopes
whistling, shell-shocked on rocking horses & dawns a
   cantaloupe
in your oubliette, unopened funny-bones sleighing hereabout
kilroys & valkyries jumping drifts of breath
original unknowns passing ignorant diplomas of warlocks
on to alien misunderstanding sealed forever 'til love becomes
   everyone
no matter how monstrous near
& deep-out we/
they are

Ironical boomerang doorbell invoking a stranger
I'm asking for my unknown name, not here, of course
echoing inner laughter yuletides breakout their hymen
    moments
rhymes on winged turtles prowl legerdemains too quick to
    frame
shelly jellos buffering against the absolutely informed
making of our image graduates of penitentiaries
not sentenced via judgments, an oddball in this lineup
refusing black holes 'singularity, imaginary diagonals
crisscross every lift until vortexes are dizzy waterfalls
mystic hysterias rising thumbs collaring oceans' smile
breathing up to voids in-between the ins & outs of death &
    birth
weightlifting jaws drooling rorschach ectoplasm swallowtails
winking night into anita o'day, parasailing with the
    mousegateers of note
bellhopping like a dingo sunrise leaning over yawn
hand-squeezing paper-dolls, robert frosted, climbing yeti
impearled by the universe now open, tracking its dark identity
living experiments added & sub-ducting waves just about
    returned
flowing within the one that manys, beckoning high
    understanding
drawn-back upon the ancient novelling immediate self,
    wrinkling radars
mclueian doodlebug spitting crystal ball alchemy of numinous
    enlightenment
riffing the whole mine, earth nursing on my golf keats,
    conventions misspelled unique
blushing ears kindling litanies, nocturnals' ding-a-ling

Nebuleum calling to echo's psyche
unknown bibles made immediately new as
flying roofs parting water in a single bark
instant mosaic disease that overcomes throughout you

glauming this lackadaisical riff, unfolding camels
ironing-board ahh, flaming names upon a tongue of sunlight
pushed down, entering hesitant, quiet, under virgil's torch
subatomic monks, chip-shouldered, dodging illumes for alive
    wisdom
off the master-less page of now coffin-avoiding samadi-tanks'
    belief
hidden within inklings' lineup, teasing deities, prancing out
each jack-in-the-box, mime ventriloquism zipper-trains
freudian steam engines throwing their lungs to the sky
butterflies alighting unsurpassed here in the wink of your
    c-sharp

Kaleidoscopes' birth in thy eye-cupped-hand
reticular, occipital, paul clay wheeling
away from mysterious imagoes' golem
erasing nightlife in a blizzard of skulls
ufos' restless galaxy signaling within
potentials betwixt not here, inhered, cradling
webfoots rub-a-dub earth apexed
loured under flowering pharmacies
tweaked, awkward, drifting sidewalks
wowing divine geometry of xmas
jerry-rigged random myself
queer for my twin I'm never near enough to swan
obliterated in lamp's dawn after your quills are spent
body curled heaven intertwined by limbo projections
gliding epicurean tickling whees from every moment
returning non-compared original unions
sailing pieces of doves, wigged by thorns' itch
barbwire quasar night's velveteen flowing electric
jungian panthers swaggering dark-plums grave-foxy as a
    blazing tree-house
haystack mind's thoughty numbs comprehended enigmas
    woven strangled
neck-tied gay open limbs racing plangent creeks naked
    drinking flamingoes

fuzzy-wuzzy mystic cottonballs, drifting like beheaded ghosts
tie-dyeing whispering undies & oracles inhaling railroad
    switch-a-rue
plot, dualism eek-swell hoola-hooping fairy-tales
leap-froging to a new vast crash-pad not the vatican
while quiet-riots in egypt are ripping the heads off their
    mummies of silence
zombies embarrassedly unread valentine the stop-signs'
    inhibition
dying of texas cyclones approaching betwixt this presence
    non-grata
zulus impregnated moment brushes whisper dark-shadows
    uncommon earth

Ruth weiss
you've won hennie-pennie too many
perceive deep brief flakes teddy bear and-some rays of vixen
    piccadilly
illusion gravitons, fruit batty omens, dame lands just north
    of the heidegger big-house, run by democratic zebras,
    trackmeets on their chests hairy as the insect priest of
    coffee- bean fans wheeze thru me, jerkwater nietzsche
    grammars marmalade spelling leap-frog detailing
    upfront internet holy breakaway thoughts aboard letters
    mathematical plato deck -hand numbskull funny-bones
    meanwhile idle wild their jumbo hearing-aids turned inside
-out thru coal mines' rattletrap or gods of the proletarians
    hiccup dance on a frying-pan
russel crowed unto laughing nuthouses' effective giraffe
because they won't sisafus up queenly kings of morning
taffy listening-booths with young-knuckles & old-nick at the
    wind-torn beach
twisted crab-galaxy misadventures hoodwinking question-
    marks' encyclical
arabian nights' donald-duck vanishing sanskrit
walky-talking epidermis-tribe-frequencies
unveiling eyeball pearls' pig-tailed dairy queen

silk-screened upon hallucinatory mirages
absolute-reflectives paper-dolled with da ja vue
ice-cream bib climbing for shasta's irish heart
albino blind-alleys light-headed like everywhichway
up-turned evolving light-switch nose-dive
king cobra medusa in a thailand flood
swimming invisible-wheels
uturning teeter-totter elbows
curving an easy hill of umbrellas
signless paraph
jerrybuilt way-down thy block
open italicized verity
thumbaleena phantom
breathing startled didgeridoos
leveling down to normalize hari-cari cliff-notes
fast-pass quick-stops elemental-ribbons unto ashes
jizomy lingerie in-between outlines' wicker-basket
casing flipped-out jute-boxes' hydrogen quote
underground maiden directions to agapé
helpful everybody
falling rocking-chairs & unbelief
dutch clogs kiacking moonshine sidewalks' platinum apple
hermit baseball time-warp catscradling yarns of thy nympho
    jellybean
with zippy doodad voodoo, unconscious iceberg in a flying
    maelstrom
lighthouse blinking odes into histories' beery ear it's quantum-
    foam
cry-babying stormy-tiller of the waterwheel universe
russeling extra-common-sense
modal wing-ding flapdoodly
your ufo pancakes distilled
strawberry freckles dawning gila-monsters
jarheads over-cast messiah cross-walk
bleedings' horizon arisen like the underground firmament
libnitz indiscernibles unidentified without
imaginations' meat-market
jewel be-gone windows

the grecian urn of smithereens
alive cinema dreaming in
naps on my jazz logic
osirus & humpty-dumpty
looking for their parts
good-time-art being huddled together again
rights for the untoward
pitter-patty jouncing up the court
differing levels shape-shifting
identical twin-angel mammalians
unknown to each-other
making hallucinatory warlords & valkeriee ladies
double at one-thirty-nine
vast tiny echoes yodeling
wing-ding ping-pong happenstance
returning to continue this back & forth unnamable-game.

Bright shadows
like electric catfish
loom from dark within
as I here attempt to small the mumpsimus
constructing now my intimate twin
whizzing random & thought-out jaunts up-late
before induction immediately occurs revelation
& what I'm able to bring-back that's warping my nerves
carries us upon turquoise stairwells to heavenly wheee
so the fire of unreturned passion doesn't consume our total
    being
jellyfish feelers over-extend immense as blue whales engulf
    moons of desire
when I depart my doppelganger paraclete, gemini-shelled by
    knights' amour
roasted over mad flesh's interior hell, I throw every powwow
    available inside the veil off the rivery curtain between us
    to make unharmed harmony flourish again, one earthling
    union, yet there's no way 'cept oblivion or exit out of these
    pressing walls of misunderstanding, to abandon universal

in-betweens even twanging the kosmos like country joe or
enlightened inklings writing me together in this moment,
lurking refulgent underneath like a tragic shadow-play upon
quiet pond's osiris wave

Clear dusk
silhouetted words
interpreted through ice & bonfires
fanged & sweating under eves
coming toward us from a page
dressed in clownish music
waving one proclamation of unknown legends
translated individually for everyone dead/alive
via sub-rosa odes only they & I can understand
non-sensual language of or to anyone being impossible
unless ignored au fond within the dungeon of absolute
    originality
antennae conductors blindly waving in your empty nighttime
a lullaby sandman of our dreams even, mathematical levels
whizzing goodbye, cradled above inscrutable vibes fork-lifting
    us all
like libnetz quantums, onto remose pluralism expanding
    nowhere
thinking snow, refining a dialectic of unseen bachelor
    grammarians
informing dr. magic, fluxing just-happens to open present
    heirlooms
grunts & cries juicing mutual equations, inventing nothing
    inert
dehiscing parachutes & shuttlecocks of batty exclamation-
    marks
landing in a tumble among the rolling wind one slow human
    flame
alighting upon this phoenix, quiet ashen vellums disappearing
    in my breath
laurel moonshine, silver-tongued, crawling to dawn, writing
    through kinship

take-offs, needling ifs to aftermath gutters & veins of
    caravansaries before hand
animisms all-over me minuscule bulldozers inlaying leys
    approaching the obsidian rooster of midnight wakeup, tiny
    feminine silent helicopters intimately rescuing
near-here buzzwords, devotee editors arriving jubilant upon a
    lake of salubrious fire
putting down upon irish paddocks, wonderfully sun-tanned
    by the birth of these curling letters, dancing on heaven's
    basement over march-hare armies decanting underneath
elementals, transforming karmas, kindling fingers, whittling
    beaver dams, swimming
throughout their dark shape-shifting, tachyons' glee, caught by
    the final olympics
relaying dashes, shot-putting periods, high-jumping arising
    lines, ubiquity entanglement's
absurd none-other hooraying the robots of mnemosyne,
    beauties' fumbling conspirators
indian twilight paraphing, delphing in womb's ancient umiak
    ee cummings' jujitsu

Ghost bunglers of mummy wasp nests
tolstoy racing flags on-the-rag in my closet
I'm not coming out your escape-hatched egg-ship war-mind
peeping up a squawk, duck-headed umbrellas are enough bird-
    brain for me
where it takes eons to get to our local market
passed lifetimes of buddha's metaphorical truth
jungian youth jiving heavy ideas non-existent
surfing in on their laughing eyes, powerful kindness
feeling before the chopsticks of discrimination walk on stilts
operating upon spaghetti westerns within nuanced antiquity
until bareback emotions ride into here-after now
sandscripting miscellaneous childhood building-blocks
tattooing diaphanous waves' osmosis-agapè
insidedly yonder than any total-cloning could duplicate the
    living ye

untouched blossoms falling apart, landing under, on-top, upon,
    within us
soft-pedaling our heartbeats, passion outrunning the
    elephantine donkey of law
lead by free intelligence, I'm bringing the whole alien shebang
    into this kind rumble
inhering here, opened by compassionate neutrality, respecting
    each such for what it is
ultimately alone, dying to be forever born, intimately accepted,
    once enough

Meta physical gal on hats' burglar wing
cuub is tic re flect shuns
dime tizzy ought ribbon across impulse
with breathing skullduggery in the ear of my cup
ovary falls in wits lifting nonsensical millenniums
looming such truth creativity gives
everything potential, nine-pin ghost butterflys a funhouse
    mirror
dreams replete unzipping olympics syllogism intunement
kung fu technocrat many-worlds dawning pretzel
salient cells membrane guardian kabala jiggery rue
wuuzy presence flooded lemon squeeze-play extreme sikhs
hide by light meanwhile green-shades dervish the come-
    around of noh-time
dictating immediacy transcendent underground as heaven
    sling-shoots its webfoot bull's-eye, xrays glide their writing
    raven, mistakes empathic cruising an ironing-board
unicycling a quiet-spoken tongue-lash flames of the brain, seas
    of the ganglia hive
passed wanweird nowhere to xenobombulate
death crumbling through incarnate networks
excruciate joy, queer dharma, looking is invisible hearing
    unheard of
return, edge whiz, jumping branches' absolute continuum sine-
    wave
kit-n'-caboodle nitwit's incoming march hare repartee

super-string fishing-poles' hobo asleep on the beachhead
marinating technical über alles, kung fu qi-gong

DOWN IS WHERE THE BOUNCE IS
Avaunt ores generalized into transcending elementals
I'm coming in on my landing uppity speechless reach
zeitgeber buckle down crushed quantum minds
hesitant void impecunious down to dying change
roaming the neck of sunrise, down-wind free of the welkin
leap mathematical vibrations echoing a jungle-gym downward
snowing ashes upon our firecracker hair, turn-down & over
    undulating grape-shot
memories' cognac of sweet blackholes, eyeballs golfing range,
    head down to the foot of your niblick dickybird inverted
    personas xraying jack-in-the-box, angular momentum
    down holy verb-vibe qizzy ears mirroring reflections' grand
    canyon birthday-cake
taking down post-office muscles identified whoaly by ideals
    you are the incomplete that makes reunion downy non-
    preference feeling utopias, random stillness, her breasts are
    nirvana eucalypti tearful jewels were passed-down around
    kola bears inaugurating a single religion, grecian urn arrest,
    nocturnal jabberwocky chocolate escapes network webfoot
    tapping down rhubarb parie, beboping virgin tree-house,
    etruscians smiling down from gravy-trains' pipedream
    aftermath, meaded down through furry holiness
vade mecum pages' bullet-proof skin-flint, winnowing eternity,
    parachuting dandelions ghosting my breath, whiz kid
    hiroshima down-under-above strangling questions tip-
    toeing the nose of dawn, illumined, traps atmosphere,
    marcel proost recalling a cork-room, downing vampire
    heartbeats, flames lapping under this grail, teasing
    amateurs promethean chain-gang mildewy lockstep
    evaporated, released to downpour
sweaty icarus, wolfing zinc dogpaddling eleemosynary
    ownership burglar twilight down lines, rainer rilke swan-
    dive, honky in a bat-cave of carnivorous wheelchairs
patty-caking away kinetic merry-go-rounds into spiral rhymes

up-close mystic magoo yin-yang touchdown elephant pintail
nostradamus oxygen landing-craft dragonfly alumni inner-
com whispering to the immortal unborn dead raking thru
fingerprints
kindling endless startled labyrinths paperclip stonehenge
before cave-man intellect grunted tides over anton artaud
washed-up & down & out again, simulacrum pseudopod
virtual onto itself neutral unique earthling clocking galactic
free-for-alls
kung-fu investigator zipping stitches down the bayou with
alaskan pinking-shears, goofy-gumdrops' monarch crazy-
quilt opens its folding, instantaneously always here, ever
long-gone-down netherworlds rising to meet the bleeding
moon's guillotine teenager quick drums slowing into a
curve-ball

UPON MY ELBOW CRAZYJANE ALONG THE SEINE
Top-spin immunology glue that deck-shuffle
winnowing no breaks
quantum ribbon of the heart
kriscringle bryl-cream floods my noggin
rabbit hutch open in wonderland
greek vineyard playboy kissing teetotalers
don juan roses thrown at me
wild as a piccadilly circuitry
zen helicopters eleven o'clock
doffing my left-out-skinny-scotch-plaid-octopus-disguise
black-jack nosebleed
holy daffy-duck's papa-vadar
elevating toreadors
slowed ken
weaned off jelly-beans
mercury quick-freeze in random norms
symposiums' chick-a-dee flirting birth
washed by tinker-bell paraphs
harri-carries' masquerade
eternal gears

keep a smile within yore line of poetry
    umbilicalled to everything
    yeasting gold-dust conceptions
    between alls inhere me
    don't be hanged by questions
    winking golems in one drunken think-tank
    round-robin yawns arising on lips burnt orange
    footsteps whisper thy dear sagas' mirage
    imaginations' animism
    before elemental wiggly pinions' dagger
      unfinished curtain's loomis truck orbiting it's asterisk
  collar
bach at a meat-market, once upon no-time
eleemosynary logic's tuning fork, walks
      inside this quaking jitterbug
      hair-trigger's tom gunn
ear-cocked yegg
upon the petals of bumblebees
zootsuit of the upper crumbs
hum ravens' sidewalk grammar
      atmospheric bag of peyote in my knapsack
lungs diving ubermitches' overdrive
feeling tall, hubris blockhead grapheme
      siamese narks, a cubism of raggedy-andys
I'm inside their incognito looking for new wilderness parties
debarked, listening minds quieter than breath
existence is our happy whee-gee
tweedlydee's dumbstruck java
licking ballistics espies its own mini-darkness
on this winding-up genetic lily-pad
vortex crimes & rhymes in a conch
ideologies peeling into manuscripts' fruit-bat
more doors reading to the waves on ahead
swimming blossoms
reflecting heaven
eschewing gum-shoes
licorice irony
hindu fun

dizzy recursiveness
u-turned within a cu-de-sac
sling-shoot harpo & miss beany-cap
thumbing you a glance

Under downtown hats
bi-clitoral toggle-switch metaphysics
traipsing cachibou
weeping library daft
holy zeros in the internet
genome erector-sets' tin man olive-oil
arcane bubble-life hiding dreams in your wave-
length, unattached abstractions writing tears to john cage
potential imitating the idealized hammock metaphor
navaho ghost-dance brushing off a sand painting

yinyang/yangyin flying van dike
idea grammar skidoo knowledge, rainbow uninformed willow
    armpits
there's lions in the punch of our between-reach, embers arose
impulse-sky, rusty downpours from the strawberry hari-carrie
    league
riven volcanoes a tail-feather lifting elevator weightless,
    alliterative
dumbwaiter, gumshoeing jainism combs, plowing with my
    fingernails
winking reflections infinity adding machine side-walking
    emptiness
move thru, condensed beyond this wind of nothing arrive the
    unending
origins diggereedoing electric hallucinating grammar,
    tobogganing
flesh walls shuttlecraft deities too odd for the hatch egg-blurt
    india,
wolfing rubber-raft honeymoons, mice playing concertos'
    grand canyon

dragon enflaming itself sundown gestalts turning around their
    diaphanous
mirror, peopling shadows limboing across from the caved-in
    glances'
image there's intelligence in our feelings, miracles of emotion
clear jinni's gungadin warlock visions sneezing yclept up a
    hindu-rope
quantum loop-gravity meditating edgewise among humpback
lumberjacks, in-law proteins teeny-bopped onto conceptions
 high-enough to skip dry-freezing islands, yggdrasiling bonsai
king cobra microphones interred in a sunflower of droopy
    prayers
haven name. pre-animisms' incognito, masks donning the
    unread fallen
beliefs of leaves, obtund top-secrets crib barbette verbatim jet-
    set theories
unheard heisenberg whispers, tweedle-dee & tweedledum
    elbows flying
binocular swiss cheese worm holes dodging their either/or
double you hairy sign-waves returning ahead, now into kick.
tooth-fairy waterfalls daedalus, tautological it of everything
jailbreak that viewing manumits own clone palimpsest in-
    between
attempting to be-both this object of unique democracy
    happenstance
subject to no law at all juggling ekistics structuring
    kettledrums bumpy
napless synapses cocooned mummy bag queerly nearer than
    here
fuzzy-wuzzy I Q gypsy numbering in the laughing plates, juicy
squeeze-play, namby-pamby hula-hoop jumping electrons
    noon of midnight
        unknown awareness swimming back thru deaths &
    rebirth, misspelling
each gesture naked hunches free as a silver-creek indian, brainy
    veins
tipping ashore your new muse roaring hypothesis, damming
    graveyards

intimate long-distance folded in thy napkin blackholes warp-
time
askew clues everyday ideals descriptions potential ahead of
the front
onion worlds virtual blueprints magnified laser-beam
hummingbird
thumbs nimble-thimbalina out-bailing braille from achilles'
grail
ivory jungles hung-over neck-choker socrates island of
catatonia
wondrous matter past tubby rub-a-dub van der waals xiphold,
kabir me
snowflaking aleatoric dharmas enzyme break-ins instant
recursive curfew
hip psalms open twilight either noir, infrared-windows granny-
smith
crystal-ball skullduggery diamond immediate mummy-wheat
apocalypse
yeast the pollen of my birth

MATHEMATICAL ROADSIGNS
ALCHEMY'S VIRTUAL WHEE
distant crystal spinozing underground peek-a-boo escape
upon fire in the big heat you notre damed a mind
italized the night with autobiographies' hypnotism
iced awake in-a-dreamtime prop-job for our new shakespeare
flying thru dragon breath, nova wars miss correspondence
v r to simulative prima urchin lab-equipment
avatars of the tar-baby dipped in elemental swim
naked make-belief river-otters on an enzyme slide-rule inside
kundalinnie high-jumps geometry falling unto bounce
spooning clear descartes written across philip glass's invisible
muse
olfactory lips alembic future immediate meme remembrance
brewing kickapoos acasshic nooisphere
declarative over thy hemingway fence
where the third eye has a ball.

& occipitals paralyzed space
freeing timeless
uncrippling east-wind
just a breeze of faith
wafts in enough draft
giggling my chimes
to awaken thee
wild mien herr
nirvana's paradox
dualism whirling-dervishes
libnitz-once verses nanny-goat heaven
artificially described psychosis
tunneling into what's begun
liquid or solid electron quark
jungian types we're incomplete
it's an underground compose
of sleeping mushrooms please
turtling all the dumbwaitoring beneath
zeroing thru every number looking for the ultimate zilch
that could be parachutes daisy-ghost opening a question
daffy-duck encyclopedia & goodie-gumshoes jetty cellular-
    sailor
lunatic wizard synesthesia hip to crossovers rainbow gillett
ululating voodoo oil-drum breathing with fire
camped under & over nova-stars while thee slips in-between
dreams alive reified both-way membranes enter the osmosis
    flux
that never crashes its addled u-turns, commingling
    distinctions'
fuzz on edgewise kinesis of tribal vibes spanish fly with gold-
    eyes
zombie receiver trump-card laughing all the way to the funny-
    farm
to see the animals out & the military in the zoo.

Oh truthful music

chirping juices
through me
hear this silence
that always is with you
enveloping all forms you make
be free oh invisible veritas
unseen like the crystals of distant snow
overthrowing all but the quiet that births you
like lovers returning within pure desire we seek
never quite reached, fiddling tickles, hiving nirvana
ultimate opium, living immortals conceive your absolute
    honesty
forever once within the inside of golden rome
are grand cathedrals listening for a pin-drop
novel moonlight awakening soundless as a white owl in flight
yet none are deafening as you
oh startled hush where you begin & end

Nom de plumes disguised as names
roam upon the mind like wheels of flowers
caressing sleep to branch the underneath you now
with phantom templates mapped imagining
sailing hiccups & knives
invisibly your appearance
night-riding opium
breathing steel
flags hidden in blind albinos' illumination
harlequins converging upon wounds awakening
reaching for all that doesn't explain
aiming nowhere, juggling shutterbugs
ghostly light-switches flying a waterfall
raining crazy-glue, quickening drumsticks
yawning thimbles, peeping-toms' split-experiment
fuzzywuzzy covering up replete avoidance
decoying the unique off its mimicry

Plump canary
under over & betwixt drum sticks
inward lookout
swinging from your topsail
its not the whole escape-hatch
its you like a wild clear hinge
opening this birthday of the universe
its nipples & doorbells
blossoms & snowflakes
fuzzywuzzy impresario
kaleidoscopic chemistry-set swimming alive remembrance
original uniques mad paddling with a duckbill
I'm serving love returns across our beveled net
complexity whistling through histories fax machine
qualia pondering wet-lands
& the evermore that's never landed
guarded by a tearful hounded clown
queer for inquiry into the secrets of wuu
touch clicks off the light
stands up to dizziness
fingering ears instrumental
persona blades wing away
civil letters arrive from the yoyo you-who
yodeling to guttersnipes' underground & deities high on stilts
there's tele-avivs on the way down
goya scarecrow dangling like a question mark
jumbo elf lifting the roof off heidegger's dollhouse of
    neologisms
kneeling to innumerable alternatives
blushing snowman's meltdown into your grail-cup
wounded dawn cradled by handmaidens
pioneering infinities where nothing goofed
chiropractor seahorse & tuning-forks' mandrake-root
righteous earthlings left-turned in the dustbowl roars
pinned upon you these notes to yourself fluttering in the wind

Cuesta ambatch
achillea neotenic

skip back, back, back future-tense
your eyes are wishing-wells
roll up those buckets of jumbo tears, drink
reflect on who is peering from the span of a photon
unknown instants that never appear
improbable chance within every between
transcendental super-egos gulping up wild desires
until all's right & nobody's left to download utopia's machine-
    made dream
icy gray hayrides bell-curving pregnant tumors thru wobbly
    airwaves
rising to burst out of themselves & spread from nothing to dig
    inside
just fast-action clearing away even old neutrality
zipper-trains grinding us into subatomic muses
voiceless among the choirs of hierarchy
disclosing forever any way out, in or between
slight as a butterfly off intimate engineering
wafting through kaleidoscopic hells & smiling knife-throws
flaming nerve-centers incommunicado
I'm null, alone, unidentified, sensitive
like hovering outer-space dust
gone whenever looked into
infinite end-times nearer than here-now
rip-tides crisscrossing mental agonies
with buzz-saws of little screams & zombie pain
only edges unbroken into violent quasars
warning me to remain impossibly tame
razor-bladeing upon a tightrope over the swallowing dark
no net in sight, an experiment of this twisted universe
individually mistaken by the nature of originality
overlooked handlebars' randomized spirit
manifold, split from the get-go, reversed at birth

Akimbo zazen popcorn dawns sleep
embracing a lock of remembrance
open to virginity, all happening once

juddering flèche or moulin
gone into steeplechase patterns
blinking lorans from transvestite lighthouse erections
swirling revolutions in a curl of your wavy navel
burning tombs uttering oracles from my saliva
articulate exploding refusals jammed before the fiddling
    grasshopper
kangaroos its leap year & the sucking mirror imbibes
    imagining
knick-knacking you apart without even hysterical plays to
    fugue
enlightened baby-powders dancing airy-fairies up to might
giant as kindness is whatever, each nonesuch whittling
    dumbstruck
suddenly like an inselberg, romance composing elaborate
    think-tanks
feelings' pagoda humming ahead, rivers of tuning-forks
    branching pragmatic's melody
stretch-limousines imprisoned in our thumbnails, clippity-clop
    your hokey-poke

Nano machines stream their ratiocination
liquid entanglements of vibe braid me
controlled by inscrutable trigonometry
finally opening alchemical kaleidoscopes
sailing through my bones upon gluon clues
pursuing fairy-tales & wagon-trains linked to reify
impossibilities winding down the fool-cap of invented extra-
    sense
cornucopias dervishing up the nooisphere, landing wide
    markets
jots behind the ear, penciling floods of claw-sponges, until a
    drunk everywhere appears
chasing timeouts skyward, way heretofore its dreaming
    transparency flies & I
veering near-sighted, mystified as thy steamroller of oneness,
    gobbling beach-balls

verisimilitude outing itself, unseen simulacrum disowning its
  fractal clones
tailoring from within obtund misunderstandings turning into
  uninformed patterns
break-dancing discontinuum's kind inertia
night's purple-cabbage raging ceasars through the mind of
  every haircut
leaking to the beginning news, amusements' unique frequency
hiding thunderbolts, napkins lifting cosmic oubliettes' monad
encompassing gestalts, skinny-dipping the acassic recording of
  once
never never miss questioning even sir ant.

Reversing a memoir
embarrassed blazes
whittling riddles
flying archetype
ubiquitous postage
before the future in-betweens
every duality ramose as a nowhere lead
threatening awe, dreading your bliss?
fundamental methods of the been-there
& anywhere hesitant like silent doorways
caught edgewise
nights in plato's cave
without a blue-green light
feeling eyelashes' wristwatch
green-gulch shadows
in tiger bamboo
solipsistic altruism
disappearing in the gone return
blacking memes upon your curbside
pirouetting totally invented alone
waking up to hum
republican atman
democratic botisvatva
entangled by quarks

medusa think-tanks
verses hercules' crib
ah pry ore I bucked from the womb
gene autrey off junk-genes
mime freezing liberty, torched
bubbling within my phantom spoon
nirvana vomits heavenly deems
reified scatter-puss landing, takeoff
from all except yourselves
intimidating principality
yet looks that fight to open
like a wild deflowering
rainbow under this passing shadow
jumping yarns
little cancers healing start-ups' innovation
bleeding volcano's lipstick
yawning sub-atomic tracks
desiring expanded panda bears of jungian yin-yang
ouija frizzbeeing baseball egg-ships
ducking an upside-down quack-up
max weber of almost pinned-down yoga
escaping here
no-matter how revised we get out
costumed disguises behind impenetrable veils
fall down to limpid race-tracks
& quantum assumptions, naked photon highways
infinite massy untouched feeling time's elastic net
marching-bands springing virgin wigwams
our last uniform taking off it's mineral eidolon
breathing ghosts' alchemy
cell-phones' jailbreak
plucking night-rays
there's an opening in every walled-up music
where particles become your gossiping vineyard
full of languid secrets & hieronymus bosch
x-rays innumerable drawing you
voodooed with gravity choices
just above tear-dropped napalm flashbacks

bullet-proof loony-bins high-flying set-theories
reason mingling emotion & snowflakes
instant abstract falling through an onion,,,,,
understanding tipped-over pyramids
nirvana mirror teasing out ganesh corners' engraved building-
    code
phallic lighthouse surrounded by waters of no-return
vatic friar bag-piping gems down a twilight road
as hipnogogic psalms weave branches in-between us all
live, complete, economy surprise-like
numinous yin-yang
decoupled here-abouts
singularities undoing
cycles into mandala wheels
gulped light, horseshoeing joysticks
riding upon a beam of the dark

CIA of the self
living adaptive genealogy
keep your eavesdrop wig on no-thanks
funny hats disguise relaxing limbs
sailing on memories' umiak
I'm a dingy to your bark of now
you're my twin's religion crackup
all knowledge's private detective
kerplunking resonant vibra-harps
transforming ethical grammarians
up insane creatives' kimono wave
tied down upon embryos' quick bamboo
awakening gentle lsd, myths cliff-side
steeped wisdom edgewise to another-face
kittens hooked by our mystic tree-house
liquored, beeswax paddling astrology feather
hoodwink queer rue murders in the little-fingers of a monk-print
what never gets together with anything except itself
instant blank in-between dumb-dumb shells
up-close there's against to follow through wit's quiver

civil dendrites kindling base-fiddles
psychopaths wheeling by aura's halo
spandrels undermining russia's mushroom
imprisoned blue jeans escape-hatched into the sky of whispers
& punk furnace tightrope dancing
indian-givers' snuffbox handshake
reaching from out-of-your-mind
nerves are ladders wooing curves
rococoed in the bottom-fishing
wheelchair of arabesque spring

When judea repaired
equivalent analogies
floated their ideas
& terror endearing to youth
grew dimples on robot kinetics
tiny hearts dipped into concrete
into lumber-shirts on gibson thrums
making up addresses' jumbo-jet
numbers' skullduggery readjusting zane gray
flaming non-de-plumes
to escape alliteration
journeys with opaque stars
cream in their vision of dark rage
surfing platypuses
churning unconscious energy
flagpoles breeze opinions' guillotine
infinitive wino-jalopy twinkles no-doze
one road-show across the creek
green shade musicality leading up
away from the spade knighthood
playing gravy-trains
abandoned feelings
internecine chaotic nut
opened by yawns of élan vital
frequencies in sneakers
crashing dove

white-tips awake napkins
quicker than your pensive image
keyboard drums unknown lilliputians
random, wild, alien, big other
nothing is as unique as intimacy
earthquake doorstep lightening bolt
helmet jazz gossiping kabala
everywhichway, connect differences
indifferent to the previous union
there's ideas in landings' amusing wing
unfinished rhizomes forever seeking their making
one not like me to be caught underground
Is silberg a byron to my keats?
or vice-versa when will-be becomes t'waz
rose vampire's lily nightingale
squeezing thru our iceskateing diamonds
pincushion cloud-burst
gemini infinite eyelash
alaska superwoman
french wristwatch open like a naked belly-dance repose
handwrting on my frig in wolfgang kitchens
designed via third-eye sidekick physic coo-coo-clock
in league with freckles & train-calls
metaphor paradoxes hee-bee-jee-bee
juggling ufos, signaling to incense
reincarnating now
I leap off diadems' butterfly
with your torch of dwarf-monks
& photon gone-awhile
enlightening undertakers
yee oracles of the diabolic bliss
eves of cosmologies' question-mark hang-ups
breaking away from the over & under-determining wave
flipped-out upon a diving-board of nuances
I'm your panther of the desert, awake!
reified in shadow, brim-down, bucking the rain
chaung-tzu entangling hui-tzu
birth of wheels, unzip your nerves

There's a wailing of sperm in miss egg-ship reporter
jiminy cricket italian verses' goofy youth
manuscript reading my ashen quotes
brailing grail, crowing from drunken trees of limbo
feather-dusted in an evening of gold
typically unbalanced
poeming i-ching ouija's crystal ball
swaggering down the lumbering plank
off-the-cuff like your hip leonine wicka furnace
bunk-beds upon toothpicks kindling a match-girl remembrance
skiing icicles' prophetic fang
di vinci gone-memories architecting everywhere
saucy rebellion in ultra-extremes of toady malts
islands' lily-livered multi-universe
waving behind artaud's toenail
yetis disappearing the never-were
chipmunk speaking through
elementals' metabolism
glowing from divine indifference
kneeling persona's leap
rip-tides in their hair
mystic veins & traffic of factories
enclosing incognito's nom de plume
spin with
virgin aches
intelligence signaling
jungian tribe karma deep funny-book
gia-matter & the origin of humpty-dumpty
desiring senses leading the mind to a burnt tongue
exiting prairies' wagon-train
raga flying hands of sunshine
circling for distilled aliens' quintessence
how the leprechaun became green.
metaphysical societies uncurling embryo's jumping-bean
zazen pins not this vibe-ribbon butterfly
as the fans' grief crystallizes into joy
& undyingly discards its spook agreement

is reality your palindrome?

Gangster kiss-offs upon the smack of davy-jones
rickshawing within outer-space
astronauts are Q-tips in mirror of distance
bioluminist rainbows swim from my wavy gymnastics
until I dagger my foot down
quivering the cabin of all lab-point minds
blues turned into ebony fuzz
sorrows of mahogany
dams of totems loosing auras
etherizing insensitives & mothball futures
pegasus in neon over windows' elizabethan detective
burglar peaches lauding open always it's quiet abyss
then neutrality approaches & bias-fear investigates me
indifference extending its dharma grace-note
breathe yourself underneath memories' dash
cats-cradling a galactic sitar now, you're havelock ellis & tone-
    vibe
dante owls blinking nod in a police car to each-otherness
euclid's here looking for his synesthesia mouse
unretired energy into wheels sailing wheels othering always
time-warp oliver goldsmith upon our front-porch, inspired
paraphing an elegy to a stoop-garden
hum cries, whistling lullabies, ghetto voltaire
POEM
misprint takes-off
your inner-skin
like an onion of einstein
feelings, dharma

impregnating seesaws
with teeter-totter flying
underneath polyhedron's gym
he-he droops, what's up on quantum cracker
icy beast fractured glass

massaging electrons
shape-shifting dragon-pad
connecting, approach

Brain signals
not pre-specified
neuro-network learning & unlearning
grounds-down our mind in physical contiguity
now you're david hume, naked as a jaybird cliché
yet what is the important judge of everyday in this whiz
    dynamic
gradually teleological pattern-recognition?
how to we adjust these light-weights of heaven?
why not compliment ourselves via dream AI
as I go-about my psalm-pilot with feedback improbabilities'
    carry-over experience
my wide-omni-range of influences, gold-digging into details,
    individual agents in the freeze market r2d2 skateboard
    detectors, universals' commonplace
unemotional maps, practicing, drawing you into becoming an
    intimate expert
situational cognition, embodied network
beliefs, where are they ?
limited materialism?
substrates change
difficult to have-not
hail-mary loves rain
every word means something different in every context
flat geometry? will we be able to program learning the way we
    do?
processing symbols met in-media-res, variety reminded
    tinkertoy's insight
levels of zetetic, emotional knapsacks, quark continuum,
    awake, there's no one
just many little helpless victim-ease gumshoeing thy
    weimaraner's quinine
animal farm in curly-qs spiraling up to extreme dawn, wuuing

velvet habermas
preferred krazy-kat-a-mount riding on my tiger-stripes in
    peppermint barber-poles
cracking this hair-brained velum like a goofy-truth would finely
    rise-up to open silence

Modal resemblances
one-no playing with everybody
dying familiars, swearing, lying, gambling next-door
mathematical whiz, duck-blind zombee celestial banking left
in a hip-trance, alphabets fractal, unnamable numbers yonder
    than pi
desert carols breathe under this hot skylight, mush fore-ward
    little townships
golem quasi-sanskrit upper-story firing-up the yardbird angel
    recording
easy-unspoken individually to you-all, aim for the energy, light
    heaven daisy
becoming a photon that never burns, up or down, island
    without kite unseen
ribbons across thy chesterfield of skull-x-rays dreaming
    neighborhood, wink movie
twins stalking each-other, building rough-trade acquisitions
    exploring out-of-duh-graven-box jabberwalkies live in
    absolute flakes like crown-jewels in neat camps, wild brief
parking clinkers twinkling from a-far-sea, duppy under warm
    arms' meat-roar
illusion scrims in the witches-brew dh laurence surgical coke
    drinking the real thing-a-ma-bob, like flying with badminton
    landing-gear? put your duck-cap on & take-the-wheel
    eberhart cross-examined by the dingbat undertaker who has
    too much busy-body addled in reincarnation lines
phoneme telecast falling tree-house broken wrist dislodged
    nanga parbat agony, odds, queer inquiries married to
    gumbo, rumba trumpets caravansary hypnotized into
    ancestral backbone sprinting james joyce, dyslexic
    portmanteau, funny ahead of me identical virgin reflection

unicycling her pedestal face armored in mercury's' crinkle-
war, vibes buzz a palimpsest of incognitos, spiders of the
internet now you'll just have to brave with your webfoot
flames lower than the unfound way down e-in ubiquity
junket over-hearing the muscling drums, no-color, not even
on the human-window-screen, gone, never stands-out
again except in his living disguise that fools hymns & mac-
trucks with swinging locker-hung feeling under their before
awakened upon windy-cliff your tresses everlasting in any
hue, blew over me zeziwit chizawitz aura borealis nova-star
with psychedelic lawyers translating apex monk on a grand
enigma with oomph darks in the welcome-pipe, empty
trenches pulse your feather-bed sailed in the cradle wood,
macdonald's deep-forest, lightening-bug-blink of air-born
x-ray gullivers acupuncture, nipple-pushbutton, cheeky as he
fuzzywuzzy isn't dealing knots heidegger apache log-house
wheeling jellyfish skeleton-keys to islands rafting alaskan
mirrors
down the immensely small never to be chained by this
    ballgame
ivanhoe on the willamette, memories in a dream-lit shroud
threaded with fates before origins dagger identity
mark your naptime, tattooing a pache(w)co

Enthymeme occasions, brilliant, relaxing with knucklehead
    uitlander's invented joy
like unwrapping xmas across the tapioca beach in hawaii
nothing rules, send a winking pineapple to my law office
I'm turning life's saga into high-coo delight kissing each
    moment
blonds hanging on my wintertime, popping dark chocolates
hip-caressing gentle wild flames reading autumnal epiphany
in-between any because or goal, sans remembrance, no wish
    to look-forward-to
bliss lapping upon bliss is happening always nowistic
concealed in the enlightenment of laughter & tears, chagrins &
    loony-bins' gypsy

suffusing quietude's teeming void, alive minds dancing up
   from gravestones' wit
high-jumping the air even intuned to the voice of creation,
   making what's presence
bedded-down with imagination's nirvana reified surreal in our
   cherubim limbs. pair uh diced
always incarnated here from satori, oh this? these are love
   whispers of blessings' abyss
vikings of guru anger, mistaken for the jism of web-sites, just
   to focus-in
buddha's quiz, untranslated from jap-town, the rainbow nark
   tweety-sweets luna hexagrams peaceful gasp mushroom
   abstraction, knee-high in elevators' deem
with cement-buckets' pachyderm weeping mac-scrooge, eric
   frome-seawater, hiring windmills' blowjob air-raid, clicking
   thru spanish uloticrous prairie-wig landscape highlight
   invisibly bicycle e-ching no-pain, finely-weaved, comparing
   jockstrap gravity twin-engine accelerating ditherdorph, bit-
   parts cutting me toward uptown, niblicking johnny debb,
   black-berries in keats, launched upon eglantine, hillda-
   doolittle tree-housing sidewise arthur raindrop loves notre-
   dame of virgin mississippi, freckled hemlock livings impasse
   the sun, big night & the unspotted panther gleaming like
   neuron-computers to the indifferent go-a-longs, decoupled
   to siamese jungian mickey-mouse, jail-breaking typecasts
   romantic foreplay psalms arise into thighbones' mandrake
   tuning-fork
jelly-roll complexed immunology, giant-fan kids the blazing
   nameless identity
pumping surrogates, funkmemes neatly track-meet, we kneed
   you, geometry handling malted walt disney shoelaces ice-
   skating earthquakes, jigs-up buzz-sawing amoeba, galactic
   quark-tangled orgasm's metaphysical, random un-puzzling,
   involutional coincident, boxed-in, off leapfrog, estrange-
   prints & takeoffs, intuitional shakedown panhandle, ubu
   inquiry greek upon origin's elastic-cake, horse-laughing
   above bleeps & revelation, whinny in guinevere memory
   vim wits, inward branch numinous rock-a-bye subtle flesh-

tones intuned even to the photon capturing groovy teacups
listening for surf-ear roaring angel-dust intimacies, opium's
golden-gate chimneysweep dark from the underground,
your leading star-nose mole, velvet's blue-ice incognito
jibe-tribes of wild turkeys' hanky-panky ten-spot one-hand-
clapping franklin image smashing quantum consciousness,
detective baby-weapons, out-with fred astair sweeps &
jimminey crickets, don't inhale your breathing-space, gusty
oxygen, junky kings & queen-doms of daddy oh, hopalong
crux, brubecking lifelines to seahorse desmond in pan-
american verse, yes it must land only then who incomes
you? elf-mask looped jinni the right-screw, yet, nostalgia
fluttering away empty informed melting unto the left-
weightless arc, haloed by the octopus vanguard chained
to smelt pomegranates, may no touchdown be my death,
I, flap-jacking haunted radio jazz-weaving government-
abstract' ear-twitter to rapids' iteration, zonked light in the
novel-turns, unique space/time hustling yonder auras of our
dream, howard zinn laid-down upon the recursive birthday
of secluded adolescence, grand-pianotissamo envisioning
the ravens' palette, seamless thimbling unicorn quasars
arabesque just beyond drifts of quantum logic, turning itself
in
frequencies swimming operative truth, improbable, yet
    envisioned
look within out, aztec moustache jumping from the deep
    buried gestures

Don't let the guess-why come back
without joking kid nihilism
second life embodied quickly now
abnormal fictions' ray
illuminates blind-sight
king cong queers first-in-lineup
a ubiquity glow
proclivities will-of-the-wisp
the never eternal repeats leitmotifs

brand-new in three wheels' uppercut light-switch
cradled by intelligence, ownership everyone
we have turned rugby's autonomies
penultimate intrinsic vacuum mustache
krazy-kat scan nap-land bubble-dreams rocket like diamond-
    tears
hanging from sap, leprechauning ecology's pigmy
out-climbs kosmology technocrats strangled by the milky-way
lucid semi-membranes australian-crawl thru inhibition
barks of glass-ceiling's astronomical ear depart together
at one h2o what did she meanwhile goats named your dark
    reflex
celebrities, flaming mind-readers nuclear-sub of the
    unconscious whim
ventriloquism mystic eight in a churchill pocket-watch bedlam
    architecture
loonybins dancing equations will rogers' question trick-riding
    gig-day sucker-punch
utopia receiving & waving moody archetypes sidetrack-
    remembering those turning-
curves, lovemaking, toasted in big sur mayonnaise lookout
    embarked upon recursive
daffy coastlines groovy-brain tobogganing muffdives just thy
    breathing airlines' psychic kem-lab, experimenting with
    irresponsibility's outnumbering reach takeoff
awed by this nervous highway, universities' teleology, liquid-
    joints dewy-decimaling sambo-mambo deleting heats of
    bleep, crumbs ray from your awnings warmed by the dawns
    of gold & sapphire, phoenixing down ashby buried in the
    last retrieval, something that lifts everyone's carry-on
poltergeist loans your mind's empathic, osmosis flibber-gush
    salty blizzard haptic reason
dashing, kick-off suicidal whittles a riddle down to grainy
    freckles on the dry-chain
quizzical as blue-pines looped on fireflies rewriting the night
    sky mothergoose oiled in
brilliant tar-babies cough-drop walky-talky keepsake
rickshaw lingering free-wheeling below qualia,

the chipmunk game-time at home meatballs & socrates on the
plato
bent neck to glom allan watts crew-cutted in a necktie
scrotums' paradise gambling nirvana womb-door
cingulated tattletales googley you-whos exchanging minds
before awareness hums numberless 'round ontology, intrinsic
quizdom
there's rolls-royces in your fruit-punch, laptop alphabets' jet of
musical's bowtie
turbaned apple-peeling knickerbockers eternity-space I'm
brailing nipples' pushbutton
freezing achilles toothbrush goosebumps shields of
immunology
over the fife of math encamped language more varied that
naked-stars
aphrodite tanning-booth winking in the click of quantum
without a still-point
zazen empty frames digging to be in the picture's noh-show
up-turned letter doing a cakewalk
birthday heaven upon my palm
quantum originals escape the roorback
kelking umbriferous yawing xipe
wu-hsin netzach toki-no-ge vetiver awol
circles jouk empty heat, decapitated sunrise
undersea flashlights, transparency without a mirror
overboard qadriyah, yerkish jujus suborn vinculum
levels climbing upon themselves via weird endearments
jig ahas, difficult groupies forming shape-shifty brain
exchanges
mammalian count-down zetetic uptake
quodlibets riddled with perpendiculars
violining fiddlesticks in the boondocks
enlightening chimeras slime over artillery
resurrected horizon, maypoling yéyé
lapping in galaxies' pseudopodium
within us all smeared cummerbunds' hotdog gallimaufry
naughty knotholes & dizzy paradoxes' unique twin
rocketing toward the immortal egg-ship

dismissive youthfulness arising from love's intelligence
jumps through whatever's underneath

Lightheaded deadweight
rollicks future hindsight which is now
scratches before the keyboard automatic enough
reactive puppet if unconscious divine habits kite
covering & uncovering sunlight bodies
painters of glad-flesh, decorating themselves
invisible moments without bankety-blank expanding
like a jungian panda-bear moon harpo flux unidentified
inventing its own cosmology makeup
gathering unto incorporated angles
building ecology over the nets of war
placing souls on this dirt to wiggle-dance in your chills
flaming mothballs' ghost just a drifting vapor
becomes a pickup-truck, quick tidings iterate
shaped by the lunar-window third-person questions
non-contradictory within the frame of honest intimacy
& agreed dialogue even with yourselves gierjessied into one
head-bumping bebop or musically preaching to the church of
    everybody
inert as a laser-beam cookie-cutting my utopia of edgewise
    raindrops' tickle
awakening green-tea lumberjack rising tarot old maid
    hastening queer kingdoms
writing checks to valley forge

Cartesian der a-dar, statistical buddha
musicality fiddling anonymous unknowns
private-eye traces imagining the symbolically real
skinny bindlestiff wheeling high urchin-pi
dangling from an oak innumerable jails
cached in weightless milk-skiing geometries of kindling logic
hallucinating dimples twilight libras ancient scrolling recursive
    endograms

zip up the smiles of the dead without your voodoo pinup
dumbwaiter underneath saucers of lamad vovs' miscellaneous
  infinitude
jazz-nose arisen thru goldie locks cream of wheat
downpour of yawning parachutes mushroom zooms rumiing
  around
edgewise tracks drifting in your up-draft ah pri-ori sphinx light
  switch
promeanean mongoosing hindsight fuzzy-wuzzy anti-entropy
infured-coats quoted live bumble-bees dot & dashing
hopalongs across the western gas-range empty scatoma's
  tortured flag
patches on a cranium, ice-cube tribes drumming within
  volcanoes' yawn
brailing nipples, areolaing multi-universes butt-naked sneaky
  peek-a-boo
frozen at the willies, virus memes spinning down-times where
  the jounce is
oblivion contexts winking lincolns in a skid-row bubble-
  scheme
mad foaming coastlines inhale your pulse digital thumbing
  away into the laughing golem
erasing the highway black-board, trusting the joy of
  elephantine garlic flip-outs
mousetrap necktie for law, framed in romantic claustrophobia
  abyss
squeeze-play mumblypeg dionysian hereaclitis bingo wild-
  piston trailblazing deaths of eider-berry-farm gorgee-porgee
  hemingway lamming sheepskins blitzkrieg eureka ipods
  insurance is no in your maw & paw-kettle weaving case-
  loads of ineffable basketballs vaccinating x-ray, omphalos
  flying-carpet alights with diadems' monarch egypt turns-in-
  reruns
teeming with here-a-bouts' solitude, raga acassically deep-
  diving for osmosis path
that encompasses the wayward crystal-flake of justice-mills,
  naked insomnia lullaby dropping eek-tunes' celestial airline
  squawking on the landing, ontology touchdown

gearshift macluein, quantum collage, shuffle-deck, yet you
    really escape in numbers

Dizzy locks
traduced vim
subliminal, episodic
huskinawing my blizzard of elizabethan wigwams signeling
in flames of invisible heat, visceral quandaries
riddled paradox bowtie tripling serendipitous numbskull
    feeling you
chucking popcorn in your diamond mirror
glucose hilda dolittle & the red swift willow
lifting bluebells joycean fin de siecle ololiuhqui
eureka nutjobs attract memes uplate downtown
servo-teams wheel-in on leaky-pan vampires, jungian radio
    early
scribbling mysteries' immortal note before infamous intell
    umps
are huxley's chewing gum rowing a seesaw on the pacific
lackadaisical upon east-bay quaaludes
fleet of virtual shoelaces' gerjeefian deviltry lit thru angels
    high-flying organic mu-muus
winking black krishna putt-putts up your transparent inclusion-
    chamber, netted by only
out-numbered paradise, dotty enough to wakeup death
Mister blank celebrated with junky dna
influenced via the kick-ass greenfoot press
your rich eyes are handcuffs jingling in neighborhood theatres
yet soul, diving unique's own launching-pad
zonky wing-ding light in marmalade
changing baby einstein special-general architecture
camel in the ray wrestling plato footsey underground with a
    bedouin
living-other modal amusing pi-sigh dimension smithereens
don't kill every word here
I'm girly paraphs collecting molasses
& sappy tears from any estranged bark

where agapé humpbacks across bach on-top
the land freaky grasshopper in the mouth of a jay-colored
    desperado
so cool he blew wit's disguise off blue snowing daisies
invisible as gin-mills & the webfoot's gungadin lapping up a
    top-dog diner's card
mysteries' cellular navy, intelligence barreling wholism ramose
    enough to be pathological lamming a split into tango
    health-camp?
I'm so burned my aloe-vera leaves are turning to fractal's
    octopus medusa
living my cocoon in ecological nom de plume davy jones
    strawberries breaking
out of histories" alibi fibbermagee & god-wally sputnik dueling
    twins zero
carried by row, universal machines scatter-brain upon our
    loopy drift adapt
seams of deems became unstitched parquets information
    radiates around to a
non-self, trances, biases, cracks from the hip, zipping up &
    down your frankenstein railroad imaginations' mathematics,
    too-much wild-honey and you're numb, chopsticks knitting
    freaks in the arizonian raindrops, piano moony before his
    fairy-teeth drunk as a laser-beam
street-dancing on my glasses, outer-space aquariums' magoo
    pinocchio nosing spinoza, empire of inverse pyramids
    autumn hills quietly nods out his vote
one public wittgenstein micky-mouse note returns without a
    squeak force
your left alone japperwocks our talk silent as a window-
    banging hurricane
chipping on leprechauns' panic, low-hung young jungians
    relaying tag
shoeshine oceans flying away in my eyeball's blackberry
    catatonia kitty wireless
universal tornados horned-beetle rising from odin's forehead
    belly-crawling wormholes time-warp ivanhoe instilled in
    pitter-patter patty-cakes unpatentable-patterns elizabethan

lyrical unreturned irony, rickshaws on deck in the backroom
with winnie-the-pooh, eeore, tiger & piglet, yes, owl hanging
to a single balloon, is this quiz not a french-kiss of smacking
dutch-tulips, zip-lock in-between miner's-lamp ump-purpled
evening capabilities draped before takeoff hypnological
naked flying-squirrel, stinger-rays & voodoo taboos bugged
windshield quilling nailing raindrops gliding in the louve
the poltergeist wily awhile smiling mid-night's don wan
rose crowned by a disappearing light climbs from the birth
of this earth, figityjibits knuckleball popping rubik-cubes,
elevators of dream-time wavelength signaling rhapsody in
hip-hop auras laurel treadmill debriefing thru my sailor-made
banana-cage no-sweat chili alphabet kickapoo-juiced akin
to the moose dubbed ganguli winks running for oddballs
augustus jurisprudence enslaves & rescues the landing gear
umbrellas folding in their piecemeal claws riffing a listening
mystery named ovay yahv what questioning info-dummies,
you or I both untogether among the theory of everything
worshiping new always mind yes, happy liberties tracking
    pablo neruda
golden pheasant rebelling flushed cherry-thumb-club bashful
    hit-list unfolds
into a roaring torch of elementary fundamentalism, nick-
    of-time santa-clause antlers lifting the uranium birthday-
    cake responsibilities across wisdom grids, cat-walks for
    dumbwaiter zombie meditation sweet-dream-room within
    the howling dark, blank reflects amphetamine jitters rattling
    church-mouse up & down the tic tock, heidegger's engraved
    neologisms, window-hinged to the stone-henge indexicals,
    landslide golems, quakes in their epileptic underwear
    birdbraining composer's treason hearsay giant pined against
    the limbs' double-crossed straight-jacket winged archery
    iridescent rainbow nightglow with a shadow-playing
    audience cawing because duchamp mummy jumping-
    bean gunnysack potato-race encapsulated distilled look-
    a-like's soul-mate readymade for inner-space adventures
    tucked 'round to feel it-become selves' wigwam kindling
    choppers zorasterism druids freud in slippers gleaming up

polished hallucinations, teachers reaching for their apple
skinny plump cherubims bleeding mirror arose kaki peak
heebeegeesbees enigma dragon-flying wonder-woman
dairyland of mailmans returning spook breathing angel-dust
orgone incubators philosophy in a ferns-fist.

Too happy to be mad upon australian flatlands
within the phantom video swimming on thy breath
idiosyncratic lemonade, deep growths tipping into velvet UFOs
maelstrom wits bellybutton armies into jitterbugs upon the
    teething of an egg
walking atop humpty-dumpty lotus flower coastlines untied
    this smile
your recaptured bygones jibbing dew, sirens' whipping-cream
fresh killers twiddling in our corncob-pipe dream eeek
inhaling your railroad wheels eyes sliding back on my
    melancholy butterflies' amour of light
to dazzle rainbows somersault kundalini's labyrinth on the tail
    of the greatest abstract
whittling ubiquity's map, comma before a lark, flipped
    imaginations playing keepsakes
timeless arithmetic winnow-souls' invention, micro-sewing
    wee-gee boards, literature aflame, casper-ghost signaling
    from her breast mid-western girth, ice-cube refrigerator
    pack-rat in this grab-bag dingdong bebop, communist as
    pacasso in thirteen lines battleship rhubarby pirate-nations
    science-fiction trolly-car dingaling all on-board, kicks &
    caresses under-the-table skipping to my future's childhood,
    dashes, tidings over bedrock handshake
sans without the rattle of a bulrush-spear
just minor-lamps' psychedelic, hallucinating reality
detectives of inner fear, enzyme mitochondria dike-hole in-the-
    bogey-average
last-chance gambling brains on a funny-farm yardbird like
    polly with a nighthawk eyebrow whacker tin-roof fooling
    the moon-rays leopard over the garment industry mistaking
    freckles sawmill escapes to living rye-grains, grail-juice

my jupiter enthroned on rocks nigh-beneath mystic alarm-
clocks, quiet digital zoa, music pauses in a hair-licks
impossible apple mild quakes giddy-up iambic pentameter
bunny-hop
in your wheelchair, jumping out in a giant cigar smashed in
your mugwumps
leaving phoenix our ashes wet into mystical drifts, heaped
with probabilities' billy-goat
tracker switcherru escapes the godellian tomato-fork, walt
disney dies of realism, quiet mostly universe what's out here
is theology inventing physic's fairy-boat
on the roar of the law while modally bodiddleeee devines
super-strings along
intuned decks of new-logic some goofball held-up the judge
cundalini-kangaroos are returning night-court handball
dribbling blackholes
go-matched to calico polk-a-dots. Kitten-cabootles sleeping
with a toy-bulldozer
pussyfooting races writing kite carving over thy alaska
toothache
diving remote mill-you capstones, kneel like a zeroed rain-
god, hair-cream outrunning in with flying middle-brows
stalled in a book longer than idling us eternity that never
quite dumbos-around to itself living contradictions juggling
paradoxes yin-yang wing-ding , 3 opens a sphere humming
quick-lines dense enough to be profound, overcrowded feel-
ups
on a trip to everywhere mapping nine veils auraed by leagues
of unknown floats
barks of terror random airports winking in from muse
dimensions I'm high enough to never land clawing at roots,
jagged mandrake replacing phantom limbo-whims
in social balance, hairy wiggles the grove of classrooms' left-
handed mirrored ripple
every pubic forest appears jailed by a geometry tigress, one-
night who yegged the nipple combination & snuck into loco
jockstrap gravities mistaken anyway, rocketing quantum
zilch, multiplying verbs without noun downtowns, safaris'

turquoise contingency & outer-space gingerman taking a
bite of mystery dawns hitchhiking to roundups of curls
inside-out bounding infinities auctioning german helmets of
dumb-skull utopia
waiting for the landlord & nobody shows his invisible tan just
kid tattoos
pulsing minuscule alarms wakeup jobs, black panthers editing
their hangers-on
symbols defining clichés lyric whiz galloping with histories'
entourage
thru the multnoma gorgey-porgy indian paths tracing in the
sunrise unset osirus
embryo jigsawing with smu, cuts-out, queer rays pinpointed
dot-com

!)!
I'm walking on goody-gumdrops so far, then a limo zips in
ss up-long as dali french bread & a jolly wiener dog, cars silent
window hums open
dazzlingo mexican chick gypsy spanish eyes picturing lord
byron tripping nature in a fosters' window-reflection
catatonia & everlasting tea-bags, nietzsche peaches climbs
out of memory amused I get-in, wrestling knitz, language
engine jinni in my genes idealing abstractions cellular with
no selling-points, she announces, hair down like a beaver,
numbers on his chest disembodied zizz yomping vlei,
flaming twees pirouette origami waves replenishing nada
excruciating mineral giants handshaking autumn leaves
then back-riding a golem crow-magnum-manikin we quietly
depart, skipping condom bands on the road-care highway
no-exit alibi transcending from a moonlit skullduggery
dangling exam bellhops & albino-cornballs parachuting
heaven levels, vibes & freaks snowing on my hay-load
numbskull toes, miniature imaginations, cummerbunds
drum in my ear, playing tag unconscious mirrory hologramic
lifting zeus-juice, electric dickybird on a wounded breast-
stroke totem, instructed with a usher hushed-up puppeteer

cats-cradling super-string's third eye flashlight rolling
oliver twist hati antiques, enter space-corpses time-flux
informative myths knew after-now all lamps & deep sea-
creatures unlisted their whispers signaling freeze-dried
volcanoes in your breakfast quakes, tinkling monk among
debugged peg-legs & jumping beans escaping chrysalis,
lighta fay under new rainbows became purple inspecting
some dark-matter energizing wonderful death unknown,
viking punk black-spider outfit housed within sweating
intelligence, aromas eve looped greecepig down causation
feather in his mao-cap, quilling deems, walls of people
experiments of this universe, imploding pathfinder-mind
in last inning's vat she was knitting my bones the sky,
unbounded infinity landing automat wing-nut flys on & off
nefratighty hardwarestore glistening iceberg rock it colossal
al cap sleep trips upon lullabies meltdown your voice & wolf
quit tall uppercut the nose-bridge drag-race cyclotrons peek-
a-boo teenage blissful agony childlike monster sawdust
forehead wagon-tongue bemuse the news lyric archetypes,
injustice sans government
ideals jailing hay

Outa-duh-box into the young jungle, whimsical as a stick-blade
    tweet, wandering perfect
catnip madness zipping Baghdad, tootaluing raving sidewalks,
    trees pruned to a knotty-fist of laughter erupted in the dark
    tavern of her mouth blinding gravestones
hinged arrows calm instilled yet not stopped dawn wanton
    oceaning elephant
upon french-horns, tailing grand canyon potato-chips' saga
    into a high-cue   ....
wheeling zizecks thumb overalls gothic forklift bracing jaws,
    karma
nite-lites' dim-train we're illuminated 'round metabolism
looking at its own naming brain-trust again
unknowable in-between the outside-within, relation-relativity
    glides

wits' seesaw pregnant abreactions she dips in her tango
 branch, kinetic quick
clocking jackknife tulips arisen speaking philosophies of
 questioning wonderment
experiential antinomies rough magic unadjusting to what
 ideally feels opossum
phantom of depth-charges smoo juggernaut creaming
 limousine whiz kid
sleep goddess bunking with high-stars origins plaything
achieve, invent creation is every verb you dolittling trickster
fooling pillbox museums yuppy ghetto ti-chee your mammal-
 glands
the earth is a slow prophet that's hymen layered as we are
 diving-boards & blindfolded napkin gang-planks walking on
 table-lands lizard beacons turn around inside your mask
templates swimming cradles zen-photo of everything's ritual
 writing
diminished fifths, jolting the universe, absolute musical news
visceral transformations garret where all lies are hoodwinked
 into beautiful
nappy freedom dreams ladder-climbing my emotions dark
 underneath a cherry-tree
invisible nighttime brush-off tictocs everywhichway to
 nowhere we haven't landed
perdurence osmosis synesthsia's indifference ramose like any
 gecko footpad
microscopic pin-drops, eyebrow vibra-harp, rushing inside this
 velvet caress to get out
thinking bali, mushrooming spaceships riding on a fountain,
 jibs away, current dizzy hiccups updraft., skippers each
 wiggle, jump-ropes rivering motions' time-line olamic
ideal details escaping the vigilant aspects of punching-bag'
 scrotums' batty umbrella night fall thru wizards' crystal,
 loopy dangling, enlightened by a yellow ghost of roaring
 flags

FLICK SUGGESTIONS

(nowhere arrives nom deplumed warm machines four-leaf-
clover incertitude)

libraries in oregon-eyes the drunken trees, moon-shining
creek-bed, hoisting fundaments of blasting star-trail down
one, shout "outa nappy-caps" (kids lying to mutt & jeff
snuffing gunpowder in some-winding fuck-you, nevermind)
mindless bat-clone of lake woebegotten oaring everything
new-old & happy-slapped & dumbfounded struck-midnight
why ain't you rich young long-shoots caressed & wrapped
(propaganda film)

then-when huckleberries saving joe-raft (mississippi
tearjerker)

80 e-mails zilch, chewing gums of kleptomania fire-trucks of
berserk mousorski-sources

no, I'm galaxy's ameba revealing orgasms twin-airplane
duckbill flapjacks' class-break

yin-yang pinball jib-sailing with easter-lilies joust in the
ubiquity quickies

wings of feeling philosophies arguing differing illuminati
stained by rainbows' bruised gypsy tailing ahead behind kid
playing lead casting your disguised meal-ticket octave

fabric's wide dna-ribbon leaps from the roaring ionist of
necessity stump-jumped by enigmas tiger-stripes muted
dark bright knuckling nephew refused photographing a
toasted ghost-dance

jerryrigged aquarium flowers

raining autumn cornflakes design

here you fool there is bank-silence

ghettos in stretch-limos' numbskull fighting tongues of hell

private abyss-space on a crazy kickball team-mate-of-infinite-
multiples

reticular wigfield zap lizards jagged sunshine orange brown in
a clown of hayward

chilly & haiti amusement you get bugging me with every daffy
mime

around rabbit ears venis-fly trap glows thru the snows of fear

housekeeping with the buddha (eraser's golem rebels from

liberty)
six-shooters yeti refrigerator goofball (lost triangle entering the
    twilight zone)
nursing halloween (dramatic struggle over titles of polite-
    respect)
kind loving without being an idiot razor, carving you a
    valentine dada whiskey honey-jar ear if you're not my-
    my-twin clone escaping ger-jeff , babying high opinion's
    skinny powwow randy crawling windmills low-down indian
    turf-jails in grand-mal seizers' dictum church-bell bathtub,
    wakeup motherfucker dingdong pigtailed raven
landing across your trolly-car spine wi-fi other maverick jive
climbing backwards yacky-yack, hear the relapse splashing in
    your amniotic wishing-well hawk-eyed embryos' question-
    mark on a broomstick listening hereabouts shadowing
    darth vader cocooned to mums' ruby inhaling harmonicas,
    libra's compensatory-teeter-totter lifts off in-taking feldspar
    whatever slattern in phantom marble chaucer gems
    kangaroo burst-out waiting-for quick-returning flames ingot
    henry david thoreau buckaroos' graphite pendulum utopias
    juggling windup upon the pill-hill singles no-hitter when
    a toaster incomes your radio-guide pinochle's a mosquito
    in the redwoods, leaves of grass verses a lawnmower
    reluckdenly, gambling a. e. houseman tutu swan-dive
    diamond unto beethoven weaves (shakespearian romantic
    train-wreck frown-clowning mistaken addresses, nobody
    cast feedback except invisible drifts & bindlestift's greek in
    manhattan ebony ufos clue in left-field too deep for a pop-fly
    highdiddleeedees' whisper tweets, but don't awake chicken-
    little or fickle dawn may-up always trot winks of nowhere
    to go dostoevsky cricket jeepers-creepers-finder-keepers
    translating the glucose earrings of kingdom-come discover
    beauties greater ampersand truth your just longer in noh-
    mind awaking with you eros & merit tireless snake-hoop
    akimbo, pointillistic gardens classical as wild robots steal
    enlightened lucky-suit's brain rich, tea-bags playing-tag-
    along blubbering in japanese
easystreet ice-cream on a tarnished-spoon, cries from my

71

hands
decks of scholarship, wackier than a queer quaker crackup
    birth dying
in each jagged line there's the raven & the microscope
    playing with leatherneck funny bones (dot & dash
    vampire-westerns done by east-coast peacenik indian's
    bullet-proof ghostwriter) camels deciding to kangaroo
    hoppalong leonine in a fountain of pineapples dally into
    shoobeeshoobe hats flying brush-off miles davis quiet as
    a gumshoe-soft-shoe kettledrum definitive listen to my
    hissing whisper tattle-tales on rattle-trap drinking jails old
    maid busted testosterone animisms & bugs in your dreams
    shmooing playdough into lucid crafted monsters' queue-
    tip & toothpicks funky-junky gingerbread rumble-seats
    yawning vociferating hairs of imagined neologisms out-of-
    context jeremiads expert biblical usurps' first draft coke-cola
    ginsberg's naked arabia pirates sailing lotus on an egg-roll
    flying carpet womb-doors machettying shredding-machines'
    infinite recursive verity, honest oddball dribbling bounced
    checks' high-as-a-kite rehired from a mantra driving the buss
    in the rainstorm-brain of a wheeling humpback aquarius
    zigzag up, out & sounding in the leap-deep twiddle-thumb
    big equalities of compassion, empathies yee vibe-tribal
    wing-ding custom mirror-genes revealing our invisible
    reels of turned-down bright-lights. feeling inhabited
    photographing dreamtime climate mime sociopath
    elephantine pushbutton conducting antennae brainwashed
    via teed-off hurricane uppercuts, slicing my left right
    down the lizard-back of alchemy safe-landing rough green
    magrette visceral response blast tickling ouches, lynchpin
    e-ching giggling into timid knaves wise contentious rooty-
    tooty-fruity
pablo neruda illusions dropping-off your toasted health astro-
    projection tooth-fairy douser wander-lust lip-sync tar-babies
    of barkly early into under-plucks marsupial pick-pocket sitar
    wrangling electric turkey-neck grip buzzards of jibe-vibe
    climbing ant-lions desert roll-back, night lairs quick-freeze
    existing as yodeling to keatean track-meets beyond inside

you & I richard widmark laming the big-con upsetting your
null hypothesis possibly by a missing straw boss girl friend
of intimidated kingpins elliptical irregular spirals wrestling
one's last breath necktieing elbow crazyhorse, funny-farms'
pharmacy underlings of downtown, inebriated wobbles at
the training-table, numb-feet jousting chopsticks upon stilts
above raving grains (hippy-dippy rip torn zipper waterfall
engram documentaries staying up with navahoing ivanoe)
beneath the moseying rush, crab-galaxy limbo beanie-cap
gurus of jack-off & jilted, hanging together ancient eggheads
in opium rickshaws,,, peek-a-booing spooky neighborhoods
graveyard crash-pad, scrotum thunder umbrellas ducking
jabberwocky mumblypeg square-jawed putty in the
greenland of endless once (trickster fantasia of clone
uniques' death orgasm in quasar bazaars tailing a gun-moll
working for the little-red-hen, kryptonite broomstick straw-
votes hallucinating fleshed-out diploma boners graduating
virgin nausea treasure existentialism rebirthing connected
avoidance you breathe upon elevator's swimming mirror of
nooispheres in a topspin. drill- sergeant wavy knitted-brows
perusing cruise in sweet foggy avenues under-the-navy
with disney in your tumblers' loonybin, escaping alliteration
truth, break-away new-music, living so there's no death in
your matter-of-fact jetty your imminence, here's dickey-bird
opening the old peasant work-shoes arendt, heidegger,&
van gohn desiring the labyrinth getaway including you made
up in this punster from surveyor awareness, ringly brothers
on my cell-phone ipods against the blackberries
di vinci rocshocs chain-ganged to a wallaby moonlighting for
snail-mail dracula's vacuum-cleaner auctioning his oracle
snuffbox transvestite counter-transference infinitude-flips,
numbering gypsy heartbeats

Heebeejeebees flutter-plane squealing to no-say
valuable queer-nickel egad running for santa-claus' coast-line
    in the boxing-ring
henry miller on our pennywhistle ignotin lake unconscious-

scarecrow wicka-wuu

burning approach curby heaps rattling about dickens near to
here-afar

mnemosyne eleuther, seeking lackadaisical inquisitive thief-
belief railroaded by the plumb-tuckered-out union, setup
by weird math blackboard sky-dust gallantry, knock-kneed
alley-bowling for the clear opaque erg laying dendrite,
instant tracks battleaxe mind in a tanked jellyfish of
washington neophytes looking unto silence, their creamy
decided weir gadzooks

alive infamous multi-bliss-a-tease, ideal octopus-mime
unchanging disappearance

proostian weather-vanes everyday a dinosaur-shift of quantum
nerves

broken-down elementals, lost sea waving home on your velvet
gloves of caterpillars,,,,,,,,,, tickling upon my prairie-arm

Landing
pipsqueak hercules
cribbing a snake-dance
barber-poles insane
in peppermint candy-canes
sisyphus dungbeetling evenings home-stretch x-ray
guard-tower walking bell-bottom stilts across recognized
lighthouse
immunology castling decartes of teeny-boppmg guillotines
slapstick wave
kindling your fingers pushbutton rogue elephants
jerky chain-mail recall jackpot ivanhoe
moony fairways, anthill series quizzing hip-zombies
tempting eringes
one feeling dippy-do woodpecker
spying on underground carrots
dawning lumberjacks & timber-wolves
embarrassed valentines quiet among dead
retired hidden in a seashell, cradling an uphill pump
desert turquoise mirrors of intelligent-tears, dripping off a

blue-fur
rub-a-dub I'm never my look-alike sunshine warm earth-
   crumbling questions' undefeated
original biases ignorant of the never-seen scrim, tornado
   artifice lassoing penitentiaries amoeba embryo webfoot
   hairnet flung around jizoms of colliding galaxies flying
   the egg-ship of the multi-universe, humpty-dumpty-
   dump-trucks yawning trombones alien saliva .enzymes
   unconscious detective peeks behind this mystic 8-ball.

Rights under the crackerjacks' om
wings in the body-meat flashing nipples on patrol-cars
transcribing hermanuetic's muse, nu laying over the sphere
break-dancing gestalts & crystal balls on the gyroscope
hip to the old-world that may not appear quick before past
   snaps your kindling
clear makings inventing fairy-queens
buffaloed & shagging a duckbill hairdo
implanting dreams of india, jiving birth to strife
laminating idling-adolescence, gimee-dah-facts
how many non-actors make just one for this setup?
whose a noh-show heretic on diamond-time
who's zilch in the next abstract
digital tattle-tails wacky cadalacky herds of the future
rod-sterling with sheherazod pearling on kulongs I-everyone
& maupassant our servant of imagination necking knockout-
   stars
entering the dark tmesis, quantum betwixt of my living mind
zippo-click reflections' quicksand like a democratic apache
hourglass vortex waltzing thru nuclear-submarines' room-mate
overhead in her auras' umbrella
nirvana beach snuggling up in ripe japanese
peachy-oranges mangoeing thy papaya on my cantaloupe
dawn under meta-morph nine-ball limbo squiggle
dippy-dewy rorshaching on this pigtail-brush
given to hymns via rupunsal, dah scat gets-out

You'll die when you live beyond yourself & nobodies along for
the ride
except freaky-geek uniques, yawning graveyards of baby-teeth
milky-ways of heroin envelops to stork-club quantum foam
when all imaginations become virtual urchin digital without
kinetic hitler
eggs on my car-door in the sunset, your beautiful garbo
delights
in haystack opinions sipping invisible divisibility evanescent in
the slippery liquid
beveling frosted tinkerbell winks green as leprechaun
kryptonite immune to maroon everything for a stay in the
disenchanted ordinary
maps untoward your wheeling gloves of this violinist
lily further hardware with a bit-part note-mouth passing thru a
cyclone-fence
exodus opening a check of my feeling-thought, happy-
machines rituals grasshopper hello copper helicopters
mitten against female-mosquitoes tizzy quick-read where's
your swimming-pool-boy yoyo chameleon tripping waves
dipping scrys from head lowered perusing the fallen rising
changtutz tao an equal spring unbalanced on little footsteps
dancing wu jiving gravity invoking pendulum's magic-
lantern leading ancient cave its waking liquid synesthesia
unto neutral osmosis star-moles looking for earthy-worm-
holes rim job viruses now just kind messengers open a sky
upon the humming brain, yawning trombone phantom of
exhaling file-cabinets, no-witnesses today on the intake
ships without container-tanks, multiples equipped to
derange atmospheres testing the racing curves death-spirit
in my wind cells sailing beyond their early jails, reflective
monk fingers spidering relay discussion in a pea-cannery
whispering in the moonlight quiet alters
idling engines wait singing jazz
traipsing into chemistries' gym
all beyond the individual I
ejected & lowering into myself
spooky numbskull caverns blazing white-marbles off davidious

thumb-sketch hereabout
innumerable wise-fools oblique frequent creeps
quizzing a squeeze-play-wall-street named hamlet in an ocean
    of pork-rinds lemonade
staggering criss-cross vampires albino fence arrowed obsidian
    to the spherical dark
balling a chain-gang hypnotized by paper-dolls link-up with
    time-space enough to infinitude & olamic your instant
    nomenclatures bill hitchcock & many lunas gainsayer
    desdemona cryonic of acasic underwear sub-rosa mummy
    guru a nylon-mask in the eyes of a baby-seal first-thought-
    boxed in via repeats smoggy-bogs damp as hollywood
    newsstands, kindling became pinochle, when velvet felt up
    the mind

Hip-hop rhapsody
jupiter saddus yuga feather-dusters crisscross
metaphysics & gungadin
immediate tracks-weaving feeling cinema going around
    thumbs
parallax galloping what could be other than agapé ?
one reified to zilch wrong button just a silk light in a jag
internecine laugh fundamentals underground enlightenment
quicksand milky-way cometh swallowing me up
while all I ghetto is thy match intuned tombstone lift-off
ballerineing star-nosed-orpheus precisely-timed to a wormhole
    getaway
confused divisions retreating into equal-orderlies, adjusting
    rudimentary devolute
improvising launching-pads of wisdom mistakes
prototypical alterity, no logical universal grand-maw napping
    julius cease
I'm on hopi-time beyond whitehead there's no now now
    forever intuitive appointments
little giant hangouts, daemons crying in the background
    multoma waterfalls gunpowder alchemy I3 I'm opening an
    umbrella, sklam, pillow lean

where origin began wasn't a quick-stop
glued to jimmy-cricketed heartbeats
clock-in pragmatic jazz
seasons of ancient rhythm
leap desert-priests fed by raven nighttime
hop, jump & skipping brooks of ideas
instead of eating your necktie or being scarfed by a crazy
    hurricane jain
nostradamis intimacy embedded in a pool-game of dreams
voices listening to your hearing completely open naïve
fighting with people who aren't there won't be hip
protozoan takeouts & walk-ins guessing baby spirits
we haven't landed escaping alliteration mind the touchdown
ouija gravity impressed ley-lines uncaused because shadows
    quicker than a housefly
alive invisible containerships permeable to unknown feelings
many genes in thy jarhead yet more honey-jars in thy genie-
    wish
than davy jones or pandora's box
action unto itself ontologically happens
smithereens lives in the church of memeing deems
juggling what's uncaught in the elfin lamp of melbourne
I'm the deckhand of your scholarship
on this ride there-where nada entangled cell-phonies mirror-
    flashing sperm-eggs from blank-check karmas dharma via
    remembrance the alive finger is my lipstick
breathe ghosting a valentine kiss upon your fresh crab-
    dumplings
purple of the purple raining away its silver into each rare dawn
just tittlee-winking to light a corner of this om
ye in-between huskinawing
enticing random genius
iterating never-over-again
this is the funny quiz

Ambiguities of blue twilight
wiggling everest

left alone as a crib for mozart pianissimo
shoebeedoobee yoyos' twin individual
virtuality reifies the incredible lucky bumpkin
unities one as no-one
wheel-chaired & rickshawed
past a lumberyard thief of metaphors
spinning heresy-hymns
billy-goat gruff's claw-hammer engramed in my femur-bone
idling meeessss jump within leaping-out
distilling a splash,
imaginary hit-man reformed by wuu
chinese-junkyard guru off hair-shirts
& barber paradoxes' keynesian field-guild
wild roostering indian chieftain
enflaming tongues
gossiping among faustian vineyards of birdland
traveling immensity
wheeling ideologies
humming vital organs purr
alienation rocket debarks
flipped out on coins in the laundromat
stamped via killer-gene audreys
neon blazing out at midnight
toasted dust
palimpsests, hangnails
rising manna
winking earth/sky
vacuuming this abyss
every shoot-up animates our reticular brain theatre
under the dark windmill nowhere
vampire picnic, wakeup!

Olfactory campfires' phantom
scrolled in tongue-licking bazaars
glacier-crashing jewelry stores
frog-prince aflame
diadems rent-a-sign

waving this orangutan sundown
questions tie-up mistaken for suicide
vagina boomerangs
cross-wired endorphins u-turn
into a haystack of gold thimbles
deep mum needling opinions
starved into psyche echoes
break-dancing nostrils in a rhinoceros irony
hip to those lying white-eyes
cauliflower avalanches
last-straw mishap
opaque energy
pin-cushioned within every reflected ubiquity
feel your heavenly thoughts iced in a glass of dogma
wisecrack clichés
exploding picket-fences
illusion arrows
wing-in both-ends
yin-yang panda-bear
karmas apocalypse
peek-a-boo unique
rumble of cascading snowdrifts
gambling hairshirts
distant as a trembling pompadour

Lost in my feelings
 intellectual anarchist
    quantum cube
     amused by the new
robots wavy gravity muscling into dark quartz
naked horsepower sans reins or digital-bit
isis pluto bucking you, erase not wit from your universe
there's too little os in the unknown known
dfehkwouypqambwoslpsaljszxido I spider before metaphors
puns for my ear-eye's untouchable valley
orchard jewel in the apple of nowhere except us
like a mystic dream

wild-honey bebop awakened
only cutouts, my hand dawns on thy flesh
puppets of limburger gland
everything's remote with this here turned around
where a ball must be sphere & galore expanded
tossing your hare-brained mind overwhelming intricacies
wedding states of affairs as a tooth to a dying belief
inner betwixt mulling-over neologisms of heidegger
veris psuedo xex
if you're a high ku
    ghetto into sagas
questing bicycle equations
                    unlike I do
Wealthy timing
howling barks of state
alien echoes in funneling illumination
phantoms drinking limbo
ruby coltrain backing unto names
slipping across enormous inner-space
upon a mushrooming leap-frog that never comes down
blending pythagorian rainbows invisibly toot-a-loo
from you, outside awes' nephew, silvering dashes in a blade of
    claws
if/thens got the nunneries' keymosavy
opening the acassic with legal-briefs
teasing chastity's renewed via enveloping mindfulness
library volumes forever impenetrably bound-dreams
awaken ye arroyos with a crying throat
dogging the gate of william blake,
there's metaphysic soda pops thunder akimbo
breathing elbows & flaming wings alight my turquoise guide
    to verities
denmark roars where fairytales return the gifts of birth
photons invisible imprisoned cocoons
winding up the future
heading mummy-bagged
shadowing past vermers of light caught
einsteinium nets whalen tieflying his-shoe down jesus golfing

brobdingnagian surf
debarking into fisheries' truth
as little mirrors looking back on us
with some weird morse code symphonies
heartfelt to escape robinson cruise addiction
pogo-jazz whirled up in yin-yang bowties
hypnotizing left-out southpaws
nothings untouchable attempting to grand-piano
implanted renewable's e-meter quake
jumping all frames unbroken into kindling swords
oceans rip within me
lava illuminated inside alembic's crucible
just a distant glow
like a freaked lion in a puzzle of j-curves
vibe-hearts gone dingdonging to thy irregular mass
yet not yet always different
indifference blind-sighted
twinkling lawnmowers off quotes
from don quixote's upper lip
mandrake rhizome
elbows' wing-nut
girth of phenomenology awareness rubadubbed contra-
    intuitive watusie
taking off your laural & hardy auras multiplying beyond twins
    all physic-habit
buzzed yiddish to a church-mouse, the economy's pulling
    your flying-carpet down-from under you, everybody bugs-
    bunnied, wireless tides to ameba galaxies suicidal hatching
    pachen up stream to escape diving into find tummy-goof
    actor who's under jive
naked dream octopus rorschach leonardo di vinci inking
    acassic reincarnation
dip awing quiet those chinese labyrinthine finishing schools of
    dualism
widen your between in geometries plumbing this night's
    jungle-gymnastics
circling land-masses drumming with humbugs & trapdoors'
    ventriloquist

jets of the idle-working-class blastoff
suspended from their own exhaling drift

Redwoods against her breast
unreturning incarnate invested disk this mad-land
hanging out at gothic funerals baby-cribs & spider-webs
crack-down awakes to the dew of the moon
just before hip racoons yin-yang their panda-bears
kundalini lean as cherubim embarrassment in a fur store
memories idling their spin-rads
built ambergris wiggles rivery
quasars, crawdad, salamander, minnow
pulsating nova blinks
verses the indecipherable clone
wake-up bedtime-stories
informant metaphors flower laughing alan watts
dark theatrics shadowing guns whisper in the buddha rodeo
pencils leading me into thoreauing erasers
szyerges toying with her mirrors; vermeer
come back through illuminated flesh
your reflection living in my wave here
like a tiny giant of condensed space
everywhichway piloting maniacs of brain-disease
whole cultivations in yummy evil virtues' petri-dish
saving the implant, gasolining anthills on noon- breaks
looking for their pekinese in egypt
where NU arcs over yeat's welding mask
entering the spirit of minerals
its too bright to face down
automobles & kraken lacing up the pacific whisper
dive, leap in the roots of neruda rhizomes
like a staggering zigzag drunk at rimbaud's elbow
gulp up your swimming pools of healthy vampires
embedded & perched just before dawn obliterates every word
    here
golems on this wheel are erasing our unnamable names
lit by the sawdust of hell this genealogy clone of 2 many

indecipherable automatons
feeling normal report to out-a-control, haunting my enzymes
wrestling mummy off-the-track, pennies into african earrings
magnifying the sunbeam, thru wit dewdrops' ubic
laser napalming cut-leaf in the briefcase of night
the flames of winter's solstice

Now I'm escher returning to alhambra
cloning paradoxical boomerangs inverted in a mobius-strip
zebra vibes become pinstriped under crosswalks leading thru
    themselves
lantern arrays of junkets winking to cupid dawns emerge from
    simple abstractions
blossoming embarrassment from wounded arrows that point
    but never reach me
entangled as I am in the completion of his quantum magritte

Sebastian bach unwrapping road kill
around about the juggernaut of krishna
tolling bodies under the spirit of flesh-wars
on endless ways & means that never get together
deacons that never come-to boo-hoos
laughing daffy giraffes in freckled hemlock
nom de plume's putting rumi in a spin
cupping sixteen pounds at the cock of your neck
leaning to a bow, one arm reaching high for balance
akimbo checkbook
wrists freed by emotional mind
wavy lens in a downpour of crying
pearling marbles of earthen golems
rising from whiz's funny grave
dingle-bat straw-vote mania jag wired
you R behind my eyeball there's a walking candy-cane
    meltdown
pinion wing anarchy start's intelligence, dippy-doing crazy pop
expect aware unique blue-suede-shoes hanging on for every
    line

ghetto's uppity our zillion off yugas compassion tracked
archetype, marooned little piggys,,,,,,,,,,, orchards of eden

Spaghetti factory beheaded tresses wigging thunder
does any ovary-gate giggling from easter improve this?
not being tabled to get within the sculptor of ideals
brush-off upon michelin rubber under you
cut-gems of jules verne
garbage truck recycling the spheres
rudimentary logic kindling whittle
muskrat arithmetic fattening twiggy incertitude
shape-shifting bark pheromones of long-living media
quicker than wisdom
contra-intuitive iron-nerves of nirvana
spaced-out at the be-in
in my jellybean kingdom
nietzsche peels vatic rome
ushering escher
babbling tinker-bells
a country empathy numbed by leather yet preferred in fur
bon mots genius illegible check-bouncing sufi
whose every inking synesthesia
alchemys you-who
whiffenpoofs that could be death
a ringing of eerie voices unanswerably calling me intimate in
    naked abstract
googleing high pitch understanding I'm listening to a purring
electronic brain nowhere differing the orchestra's quietude
whispering rational consensus entangled in touchy quarks
gnostic flames via dark razzmatazz
born in this hilarious heart
weeping unto nada glue
investigating addled tears
pioneering ecology's recalled oxygen-tent
nazi boxcars jiggling open
escape my veins & chirp

Tangerines awake san francisco
witch-cap switch-a-ru
those knives out the labor of your back
let the hindmost translators question jitterbug
collaborating newspeak knocked out by the amused muse
jock-strap shock wakeup between dreams
hang-glide cradling every land
where a sparrow owns a gas-station
& runs the hydraulics with its giant pecker
lucid belief skips to modal necessary ifs
ant-flying jumbo-jets with adaptive design
how do you program something that's live?
not-easier I've learned via fantasy
where scrims go-round the horn
under the keel of psalms
there's a wailing of sperm in miss egg-ship reporter
jiminy cricket italian verses' goofy youth
manuscript reading my ashen quotes
brailing grail, crowing from drunken trees of limbo
feather-dusted in an evening of gold
typically unbalanced
poeming i-ching ouija's crystal ball
swaggering down the lumbering plank
off-the-cuff like your hip leonine wicka furnace
bunk-beds upon toothpicks kindling a match-girl remembrance
skiing icicles' prophetic fang
di vinci gone-memories architecting everywhere
saucy rebellion in extremes of toady malts
islands' lily-livered universe
waving behind artaud's toenail
yetis disappearing the never-were
chipmunk speaking through
elementals' metabolism
glowing from divine indifference
kneeling persona's leap
rip-tides in their hair
mystic veins & traffic of factories
enclosing incognito's nom de plume

spin with
virgin aches
intelligence signaling
jungian tribe karma deep funny-book
gia-matter & the origin of humpty-dumpty
desiring senses leading the mind to a burnt tongue
exiting prairies' wagon-train
raga flying hands of sunshine
circling for distilled aliens' quintessence
how the leprechaun became green.
metaphysical societies uncurling embryo's jumping-bean
zazen pins not this vibe-ribbon butterfly
as the fans' grief crystallizes into joy
& undyingly discards its spook agreement
is reality your palindrome?
while crackerjack dawns
high-cliffs are oughts of autumn
wintering lucid spring-rolls
enfolding time under-arm like a pigskin on a yorkshire
briefcase quicker than forever
clarence darrel kindergarten
paradoxical tautologies' antinomy
in-between thy meme of dreams
vision yawns
white-shirt on the night-surf
& letters glide tides of our milky-way
smack enough to repeat future postage
numbering the big-con & truth's incognito
Is silberg a byron to my keats?
or vice-versa when will-be becomes t'waz
rose vampire's lily nightingale
squeezing thru our catdoor
matchbox roach-mobile
pincushion cloud-burst
gemini infinite eyelash
alaska superwoman
french wristwatch open like a naked belly-dance repose
handwrting on my frig in wolfgang kitchens

designed via third-eye sidekick physic coo-coo-clock
in league with freckles & train-calls
metaphor paradoxes hee-bee-jee-bee
juggling ufos, signaling to incense
reincarnating now
I leap off diadems' butterfly
with your torch of dwarf-monks
& photon gone-awhile
enlightening underground
yee oracles of the diabolic bliss
eves of cosmologies' question-mark hang-ups
breaking away from the over & under-determining wave
flipped-out upon a diving-board of nuances
I'm your panther of the desert, awake!
reified in shadow, brim-down, bucking the rain
chaung-tzu entangling hui-tzu
birth of wheels, unzip your nerves!
When judea repaired
equivalent analogies
floated their ideas
& terror endearing to youth
grew dimples on robot kinetics
tiny hearts dipped into concrete
into lumber-shirts on gibson thrums
making up addresses' jumbo-jet
numbers' skullduggery readjusting zane gray
flaming non-de-plumes
to escape alliteration
journeys with opaque stars
cream in their vision of dark rage
surfing platypuses
churning unconscious energy
flagpoles breeze opinions' guillotine
infinitive wino-jalopy twinkles no-doze
one road-show across the creek
green shade musicality leading up
away from the spade knighthood
playing gravy-trains

abandoned feelings
internecine chaotic nut
opened by yawns of élan vital
frequencies in sneakers
crashing dove
white-tips awake napkins
quicker than your pensive image
keyboard drums unknown lilliputians
random, wild, alien, big other
nothing is as unique as intimacy
earthquake doorstep lightening bolt
helmet jazz gossiping kabala
everywhichway, connect differences
indifferent to the previous union
there's ideas in landings' amusing wing
unfinished rhizomes forever seeking their making
one not like me to be caught underground

Pouts sphincter wrinkling quivers
estranged return boomerang dingdong
meltdown to the basic-elementals
ideals fanning pascal & boxcar's insectitude take off into
    literature
then wildflower up gnosticisn, snorting bullfights' hemmed-in
    watch-fob
eleemosynary universal pause, remembering your divine wino-
    question mark
joking tricks arithmetic, laughing hegel, beheaded, tossing
    isthmus mind's scared revealing paraph everywhichway,
    translated future amanuensis devoice whispers investiture
heartfelt thinking ought-not aura jiving irish enigmas,
    responsibilities' unmade-up pubic-forest lariat jib-sailing free
    of this goodbye baby-pie, enter your inner-dream, jack & the
living-room theatre recording de ja vue yummy quiet
    installment, christ & self-help marry italians give-up their
    black flags, crimson hamlet skitz, dialethic logarithms
    kind auto with yep infinity relations, a lincoln penny sent

east/west of dundee forever warps the parabola acrobat,
calculus on quasars, huey newton barcode jitterbugging
skating-rinks with the redding gaol, escaping thru dewdrops
invisible mirror looking at itself smithereens beveling
lowdown to the juicy fruit, I'm tan alien queer universes
wink hindu neck-chains crashing my sleep, rational kid
loaning an orbit
peeping at the unheard, listening deep-breath
night-ushers dangling the easter-egg of the moon
fasting like a hermit spiraling umpire omnibus
distancing into july's russian circus sky
austere gangster hip-hop, knife-throw tarot
nondescript, mapless, riding a daisy, wing in the oaks
humoring around the blind-eye of every storm
velvet jails curling zens' inner palm
dwarfed solitude condensed in a wild orchid blush
handel rebellion dying liberty
elizabethan morse-code doting the night-sky
blunderbuss spirits parachute
iambic trained windows flash & blink
you'll always miss once your everlasting
jisoming smu, dealing new kleets
goosebumpling along heresies' braille
kissing thy smack
i'm dizzy acupuncture mumblypeg
intimate giant-toed upon foghorn oracles
bell buoy in the kingpins of dante
swinging alums escaping lightfoots
rustling-up a bushel of glowworms
night ping-ponging constellations' yarn
info-myths drifting breezy evening, tanked on holy mud
listening in my cups, geigering distant jerkwater, thumbs
    raised
I'm naughty knots phantom of before, limbo gestures around
    thyroid's ray-gun
fingering inferno hermeneutics underneath the jazz muse of
    bach
squeegee lsd windowing yonder pi union novelling continuum

random freak with her dousing tunningfork pierced-tongue
   snake-eyes roll
bone-scrolls living fiordic giggles, whittling intimacies' origin
   milieu
herer than near, tombstone dentist, elbow-winging down the
   slopes of afirca traffic
perkadan on my back immersed dreaming rooftop
quiltless sinews flowing in the milkyway's lingerie

Walk-in, toasted, eternal billabongs daffy-duck under the
   recording
haunted over-wave supervient from the nether kaa
lever mobil apple-core eschering us insurance high-rise your
   terror browser
iterating unique repeats flimflam condors glide big-banging
   multi-universes
landing alike flower-blossoms hum of emotions periodic table
   instantly ruuubkic-cubed
skidrow conch digital jump-rope metaphors grin awhile
   boatswain ideas widow flag
eagle recherché yird twilight abstracts dawning invisibility
   cage poverty bliss
opening equations' gestalt now the unheard tweet rococoed
   hereabouts shadow-
boxing charismas infant antinomy feeling a tamalpias owl
   doting the upper-boughs
molasses night wakes breakfast quicksand omnivorous askasic
   galactic sponge-cake
harry beaver against the duck-blind web-foots, caresses raking
   microscopic life
juggling gee-whiz ecologies loaded with alliteration, nomadic,
   eyeballing
through marble rivers heaped-deep with smadhi jewels'
   drunken aide
lucid virgil popping raisons from the crazy grapevine elephant
   blues-band
archetypes spooning out my basement reincarnated personas
underneath the mask, heaven's fantastic imagining, entailing

non-contradicted recursive paradoxes' somersault tumbling
nerve wiry dramas yinyang
orangutan inebriated sunset death winking egypt never-landed
uncle ben

Here's a respondo to yoyo pome dangling before me like a
spider climbing into fireworks
stir-time was nowhere when ye weenie-roasted preachers of
another
claustrophobias differing smothered via lettuce outing within
raunchy lancelot
hen-kept reaches would long for the old maintaining tight-
reins' unconquered agony
dull pancreatic ectoplasm go-games estranged indifference
cursing well-wishers
mandala's front & centered auto-jack off u-turn evolutions hit
by a nap of disease

Lobbying mugwumps
vacillating clear-thru wise greece
whether I'm signaling puffs or fencing thumbnails
dancing elites mailing winnie-the-pooh
alls in the istigheit bumblebee
looking for humes dark-hole
deaths not coming without a period of sunrise
leaping underneath gestalt's twin
your more alone than you know
wheeling voices hemingway abnormal blew the sissydom
flesh oomphing auras of vanity aren't you more than one
bleeding music, whiskey dugout, funny across stagehands
relay teamwork cooky-cutter tracks the embreo who-dunnit
yummy ibsen greenfoot daffyduck laughing off bleachers in
her rooster
white-chocolate skull, miscellaneous quip, eternal politics from
a weird time-warp clock
arrows winnowing everywhichway freights of delight
glauming auswitz entrapped lucid rivers in my eyes jets

upon stevedores of concrete-dream
elizabethen irony in the brain of humor
marbles playing with too-many nukes
inebriated hole-in-ones with the venus-flytrap
transparency no-more always veils
auras of poltergeist jewelry
martini, bellybutton, lala deep shadow

Transforming your apex, exploring the nerves of our
    underground vineyard
impolite respect cherabim adoreship & jellybean ovens
    anagogic, nonpariel
loquacious mumbling invisible silence illuminates thy snowy
    crown
warm in a hairy-tree playing oranges with thy little-christ
your kitty on a yoyo antic yates chick dark gallium
skin firey as a danny kaye lipstick tongue volcano
illuminating nitwits woven into donkeys of mockery
clocks taking off their inside frocks
revo-invo-evo-devo questioning an embero
then it's us, pumping out impulse
gravtrain mentalities
amnesia, boomeranging one weird-knot
jamis vue revueing de ja vu
super-nova kiss-off
ennui aboard to the funny-farm
plowing wallets
stitching handsome daisy-chains
winking dawns
alien night machu picchu
tippy hypothesis
we're cradled by the dark
slouching universal brubrecks' sandy warthog
sua-sponte, I'm a robot helping wishingwells
fleeting oocyte armies goofy swipe newtonian
dimmy-dimwits torchflare into caves of bleeding rivers
jimmying pulse saved by a digital star

web to the metaphysics' psyche
inter-weaving chemistries
we're carrying endlessly ipse
drinking from the ear of my tree
home to the overpopulated sparrow
thomas hardy chirping on my line winter's joy
up-late in sighfy doing breakfast for the mark

Street-value jumping caps
guitars of unknown disease
audience cheating out foveae
instant silly window goose-down
hari krisna asthma left my happy errand
burping thunder, finny-gunsel missing link
navy strawberry qizzyland break
here's tiger junky russian wig-tent
gypsy egypt in rome, stoned by mix
a lioness from the wizard's ozark
dipper li-po zilch, racing moans hiccough
in my flash of paddy-wagons
smiling with grim amigos cornering a frozen nap-dash
twins apollo, binaries of love-wings get together with their
    queer farris-wheels
rating on neo-religion shadow without phobias
clear as a virtual mirror transcripting to you
distilled alembic blinking lincoln in my zippydodah
valley spring-blossoms bella identity hip
one dingdong communist fiddlefattle tightrope
a ghost lamming a powwow once a jamboree
dust-powder the whites of their off-sides baby-dance
virginity mistaken for ruth weis yin-yang-ping-pong
remember your network elbow-wing
germane trojan,.escaping sky-dives
of doves, hitchhiking this crystal blizzard
walking just before afternoon
tossing yesterdays tossed sleeping in meme-waves
undercover with the infinite palimpsest

dinging cash-registers into nova-stars' wink
sweat from a dark boxer's head .

Necktie peppermint question karl marx
surfing cocteau
hanging quits
committing lassie-glasses tizzy-faire
giving mind to the holy rabbit
ledges, arc-lamps of green encyclopedia
vessel sorteries gimmi-shelter by your cradle
the identities' pollydox whip-crack
in the jungle of fear, voices, hunger
guruing within the pleiades, anxious now
whirl off swift as the nowhere messenger's address
its ye stem-cells to relight the vertical libertarian
systems parachute your rocket ship
bypassing jesus across thy insect straightjacket
fiddledeesticks enfolded-up museum's zazen
aphrodite slipping between an earthquake & a typhoon
meme-feeling, drawing the brains of heaven
this is what jiggles about goswammi
networking the brahman webfoot
there's ball in play & heshe's into dusting advice
scrying upper-mirrors, heartlands empty, gushing sunburst
    butterflies' gallimaufry
kinds of time weeping ears jingling leit motifs washing away
    to neutral one reflecting survival revival crazy witless
    awareness birthing miraculous envy, ANGER jealousy PALM
    IN PSALMS WITH FEARLESS GERTRUDE NEWS SKIING
    DOWN A JUMP
neither saddles raining teardrops dante hot-wax wake pastel
    gorilla
buffaloing kraken carol heronimus bosh tide-pool eyes
flippant omi-bust, startled buy-ups wanted originals
listen to feelings if you're not masochistic, don't punish
    others anyway except in an open pun become intimate
    with yourselves, take in dusty angel inkling leg-cast mid-

western blabbermouth indians raising quiet hello flying my
unconscious spontaneity, misspelling early here digging
your birth

Speedy mud
universal chum
on what level duz
questions desire the return of return ?
dante hang-gliding
perfect touchdowns
lashing odysseus
skipping the mineral eyes
we dived inside-out
jeeping the hills of her curvature
sundown rising like a golden-grape
timber fall echoing thru jaded shadows
why masquerade dialoging gaylord's parade?
the pollyfrenic sad-clown of a kid's mind
natural gates evolution would-be bush?
answers coming with questions rococo
laughing daffy in the mint-print wakeup
repeated underneath enough breast-trembling romantic
    guesses
hari krishna's strapped to a pan, tooled by the big dipper
    wuuing you-who
each is always too much, piglets a talking ear o I dig thy limpid
    olympics
byegones gota-run-a-long same dear venice minuets coming in
    new animal farm dogma
gone bezerk on equality, generous as a tightrope skiing on a
    razor diamond mine
choo-chee-coo tendering the hand-in-hand arms-race with thy
    moll flanders
lamming pepperdine & safe-harbor goals my beatrice from the
    deep
cracking knuckleballs give away to the waves sideways
    undertow

this morsels out to seal our questions gone in petro-electric
   transparency
disguised economy sleeping with muses' fecund birth
out-numbering too many numbers in democracy jails
googling chinnychinchin darling into one neurological blues-
   band, umiacking a ray-boat
delouze & wittgenstein in the grand-piano ebb of your sudz,
   climb onto moose-tippy-canoe
each level is heavenly, this path's not-taken wrecked by rents,
   strawberries with the measles
busted eye-glasses off a giant african twig-bug with iceberg
   tears
crazy-glue particulars about to explode, take away the lock-
   step tic-tocs, be the flying reverse
ho ho drawn by irvine ladies qued up ahead of the
   miscellaneous somatic brail
when teetotalers inhaling drunks upon roller-rinks kitty-cart
   your candy-cane, get on lamb-hook skates, metronome
   bebop hopscotch, gum-erasers dusting sweep before the
   anathema waverley novas camelling quasar bullet holes
   daylight no longer frowns upon us
meandering durations' rainbow, climb out from jazz
   pragmatics
stepping on it's trucking rehearsal with invisible dreamtime
film your stereo, unreturning the long-gone drifting ambiguity
   pincushion
winking cosmic truth in the silence off a falling, limbo leap
rose-petaling aflame beyond its matchstick
wing-dinging in deep galoshes of night
jerry-riged unique -----

Velvet gambling nocturnal diamonds, sweating fisticuffs, radar
   wrist-watch v-day
long-gone event being occasions x-ray jungian cellar doors
   hingeing whims of teraphims
idling proletariat archetypes no weaker than brand-new
   shelly-bugs lifting neruda's flying rugbe team meanwhile

clothespin pelicans trim my irish sea, trading look-abouts,
cookie-cutting your gothic barbecue heretofore, up-stream
in alpha-waves, quick ghazals' shimmering cross-walk,
rising eight-ball knockout, techno-sleep bowling egyptian
mummies in thy avocado oaring the jungle
immune to everything, ubiquity-ringed via fourier lemon-drops
& rudyerd kipling leopard-spots
hung by constellations' trolly-car & rainstorm jalopies, voodoo-
stitching up a dragon's spine
tilting, heady, for ye know-not-where maybe here-where I'm
nowhere thumbed beyond these instants undoing this to
be a lefty so to be careful with the stamp of a moon-dance,
illuminating rocky-roads out-spaced in jellybeans, scatoma's
eye-patch, flag-waving virtual junkyard's impossible akimbo
unto gesture's of beauty, lifting off, kerplunking down the
snapdragons' opium escape-hatch, bellhop instructions
claw-hammering zippy islands' did-o-data, humming loony-
bin friendly, trailing camp-grounds thru an opaque alembic,
under the weeping sea-crash
konks of black-white yin-yang anger peppering in my rapid
currents' impulse
novelly didoing itself, mathematics branded by a synaethesia,
origins jam
industry cuffed up with knelly belladonna flowering the walls
patterns of random longing, what happened to good-times'
social capitalist with extra-quarters? armband, tow-truck,
don't be linked to my hang-ups' question mark
unless wit grins childlike yonder intimate pirate sailing this
master-less lily
nova angels' dragonfly pondering each correspondent's happy
return
tuneful notes, slouch-down in a wild forest, crew-cut & kung fu
your recycled handlebars
while hidden from justice, purples gingerly dawning into
mauve

Novelling your de ja vue
quizzing its fish-net of cats-cradle
weaving guru mummies in swaddling-clothes
helicopters of japanese fandangles' unknown legend
the raggedy-andy flophouse for dead teddy-bears winking
    childhood
sprinkling reindeer jasper-johns grand-maw imprint
the pilot-light of outer-space teaming up with in-between
    mazoogonah
neutral buffers stalking jesus
caught on the dwarf-web
hiiididleedee

If its so much of a giveaway, you forget & what you know
in all the dugouts of your empty abyss of liberty
nada doesn't showboat this catwalk math
now purring in your fiefdom
thinking multi-grains on the wing
roaring bathers dither sunlight freckles
rainbow philip glass ears of washington carver
tomorrow blinded via flashbacks
hug the line immediately
non-awareness
subatomic examiner
gilded over by the meaning of willow-bark
always printed inside lures objective grandeur
enflamed tattoo praying to non-denominations
stowaways gambling duckbills raining in the autumn flames
climbing ironies sine-waving arabia
originality vanishes inwithin the heath
disguising echoic quotes whizzing through my underwear
pilot-lights & matchstick boxcars, niblicking a hurricane
caught in a tower of reflection, flowery phantom kindness
hits like pooled anemones slowly exploding your last nocturnal
    tic-toc-tac

Talking to jesse red pond
his rigaletto insectitude electric bunnyhop kickapuu nearbeer
in your earshot adobé
a zzillion gunadins ahead of the sorcerer's concrete numbskull
many afterlives by your elizabethian liver world-touring the
amateur of promethius, undiffering infinities get-around
save & delete parachuting trypodal visions where the
bounce is
cradles enfolded within our making just then strange invisible
window hail-storm
awayed me ravens alighted upon my foothold sleeping
iridescent in your dark halo
laidback like the dictator of ease, winkum, blinkum & nod
check for the spooky-spokes we'll write them in along thy
googols of indians on our virtual tabasco-sauce, it's the
moe-show spelling bee of equations fabric your adolescent
elephant out-running bout into wall street leonardo di
vinci on an anthill of rorshachs numbers shadowing your
phizeeogname wiggling a flash gordon zippo, , oola light,
trenchcoat chick-a-dee get the weighty-ribbons to speak
this fall glassed in membrane's elevator, immpermamable
to imbibment of one time-flow, passing between-times
personas of each now-vibe, ahas merry coming teleological
duncecap on an upsidedown vortex , the feather riverbed
who never lands without a skip everywhere's your reified
dreaming memes, cooled by icy sadness walking tattoos
idea dippy-doing in his baby feet, greenblue last-down
huddling with the cheerleaders maypole dance screw-balled
toulouse latrek in kosmic fuck eternal bit conducing by a
mouse's tail in-the-middlin dialect when amphedimenes
bulldozer hayrides living on bamboo fluky flutes raffle with
mark twain will rogers & waineo drunk camel teat grail plan
before your errors run you in unto you
third degrees not peachy, nietzche

Sucker trumpets, achilles, wading vessels of hair
nevermore un-revealing this profound contingency

arguing the microscopic raven of poe
tickling sunday-punch hiding the familiar
wild crabapple scaled over dyes of light
alive in the far-away off kissing eyes
rehearsing the future afterward before
multi-dimension leveling my gangplank tongue
a wagon-train looking-out notebooks unending sky
retouchable massage whispers of the dead ahead
vampiring immortality each pore a hungry wave
grazing cellular urchins' feckless jupiter or peoria I couldn't tell
    which
rye-bread into ashes pad-crashing take-offs
omnivores' carbuncle lighthouse ray chandler
wireless strawberry akimbo
freckling dot-in-dash paddling in on the new moon
strangling umbilical granny-goose amused
weighed-down by rinky-dink
in a marathon with my elfin-selves
logical jam to simple for I am that I am
experience broom rug nice the quiet meaning of you
depending now on-how we're reading it
here is intentionally left-out

Staggering leaps
tucking-in a photon flux
my golden-lionness appears
trailed by fibber mcgee & molly
cagey hardware-store jerry-rigged kosmos
thinking-aliens reaching for the homeless launching-pad
upon weekdays muscling zarf, imbibing unknownable
    universes
near-sighted here spy-glassing for wit's grail-queen
like a broken chipmunk tinkering a star-ray
whitening nighttime hoodwinked, moonlighting a tin-cup
kellogg cereal yells echo across tables, dawning alienation
ghouling high-schools down unto bounce
that once ruled the fractal-bark

bib-scrolling electric pianissimo
lifting a mind quizzing wonder
the only reflectives being the carry-a-ways
goodly single hand-clapping liberty
ding-a-linging this buzzword
flying us, elephantine ovary nippling pushups
watch-fob quivering thru heats of the invisible vibration
tribe at ease before shadows descend upon our inklings of
    night's caress
purloining all minus the landing-gear
I am not yet I am your nonbeliever's belief
eensy-weensy majorities' freaky's unique
old-growth into tinker-toys' pregnant heart
erasing this golem upon our dieing/living freeway
don't turnaround philosopher
reasoning's out with quantum switchblade
whisker the light in a curve-ball, de ja vue
unfree gratis-leash blossoms never fade
plumbing your mystical dungeon queerly castling a weenie-dog
    stretch-time
each itchy-bit living on allah's brown twilight
rising in night-voyages 'round drama blocks of evening
with dewey-decimal's rip torn voicing-over new conservatives'
    antique whistle
spell flying in upon the breathless wind like a milk-bottle
    spinned no longer by rumplstillskin's nameless game,
    pussycat chats socrates, her uphosteriy reincarnated via a
    mimic clone-machine into ghetto scratch
punch-drunk on a french-horn breaking away from oprah's noh-
    show
lean-too slapstick, eeore-jazz withdrawing from the democratic
    club
gidget no longer pushing me forward upfront kennedy who
alighting with tanned-reporters, eyeing the dark love behind me
shakespeared light, income roaring to a listening sandcastles'
    whisper
crystal sea-creatures reasoning timber-roads
grasping a will-o'-the-wisp heaven that'll network your mind

SLEEP

It's taken me years to get five hour-shape-shifting upon my
    left-side
unawakened by immaterial memes commingling with
    southpaw eternity
dream-tripping bedowin, wrapped etheric auras underlooking
    subtle outa beeswax
amber thru yippy-yugas of creative energy gandhi housed in
    your traveling veins
becoming of becoming penguins, maenads shredded aches
    take on fields I caress
wakes of ideas estranged hoopla dashboard radio expand
    appealing manilas of vasya light
cells put wind-a-hymnal sky-scrapers glass elevator nembutals
    you-whoing down tooteefruitee anybodies-homerun lacing
    up your facemask rational snowflake kindling unscripted
    yelps, exuviates taking off infinity daring, leaping cotton-
    photons tripping bushwhacking Gila monster undercover
    mescaline pok-a-dots yin-yang beany-cap lands uturn
    rebirths off science tumbling from parachutes monk granola
    jawowki cymboling ivan the terrible aluminum, luna noir &
    in-tune tony looking for oscar wilde junkets giggling peace
    floating cradling the kulong bay & picnic upon dimmy-
    dimwit knolls immutable yet liquid spy the inward mirror
    of you reflective jinxing our unreturned quest gumshoeing
    an ion, tachylons seeking enzymes, adding-machines of dna
    hits, voodoo raisons bonzing weeping-willows unknowable
    beneath the in-between gap-tooth laughing cemeteries
    typecast vanishing in a baby-grand, jumping the entrance
    oding death, reincarnated as physics' zombie-making
    lines in a quasar keepsake notes I'll jig you a way to many-
    selves reincarnated terra-firma popcorn diamond in the
    heaven of winky-blinks psychedelic spittoon late motifs
    googol childhood, justice is a membrane betwixt the the
    next funny-world alive unbalanced rd lang coming around
    in my wild arousal you're my dervishing bumbling halo
    goodbye embarking with my silly alligator blind nose-cone
    osirus dick for what is unsettling, characterizing personas

like god-wally-sputniks, nightingale bruised exploding
universes omnibranch axioms nervy enough fractaled
into math beyond compute random winanims pipsqueak-
barks to living afternoons, oregon deep in gray shores
embarrassing the cherubim's of winter-crashes in the eve
of shadow news-stands a muse, private detective ganglia
ubiquity beantrip sanskrit abacus into wooden dingle-
berries forget votes electron rorschach's sew your naughty
oughts upon a transparent yacht released from go-go tree-
house clubs batter at the mark non-returning race-tracks
pubic-forest exploring aprizments mothergoose lamp within
kleptomania hypnosis umiack gangbang forgives me smack-
dab cadillac trickster gleam ecology wheeling fiddlestick
dendrite avoiding zen lamb-chops cry-baby octopi medusa
brain escaping its thinktank redreamed in vines quivering
an open window to dante's taxi fare, galactic pinball rabbit
ushering dizzy windmills arrival launching-pad dare-devilling
nirvana's' many-world envelop, knapsack-abyss
cocooning the mummy of baghdad.

On letter & number 44
robots in the bleachers
zeal I'm hiding in my jeckal
default mode networks its skinny inside these wordplay
    quickies
under the luny-screen, a flames inside this haystack lion
    escaped from heronomus ozwald
a tickle eternally drunk wipes itself across butcher-papers of
    bach
swiping kleptomaniac miss orange-hand grips caliban
    babooned auto-de-fey
tapioca rainbows, india kiting a check-up hanging-with winnie-
    the-poop-time
energy is created by our brain differing nude-whistles out-with
    musket-balls in them
policed by tweety-birds infamous as a rising crash-pad
    lamming the fleas grew to be

giant seraphims parachuting ice-skates into wonderland, de-a-
  tease becoming unglued
struck-dumb in a laughing igloo, helmeted upon washed-
  up accordions & metaphysical road-kill giving klap to the
  audience, immuned by this pocketed-rocket illumination
escape-hatch glances, signals from oddball kinetics, ruling the
  big game

Anything's what isn't here therefore near engineering intimate
  approach
impossible realities labeling names in the bee-business
  jarhead, dented to spin-rad
necessities are your caboose zonked via multnoma-falls
  gorgey-porgy wakeup umbrella
huffalump away rat-cage daisy whiffen-pooph sun-dewy, lit
  tobacco questions veiling ghost-writer, high or low, there's
  fire in this sky-diving like a cave-swallow into your musical
  enzymes launching wit's memeing dream-job retiring unto
  funny-bone belvues' healthy-spell, cradling everyone on a
  low fire under their dancing thumbs, omar kiam, rebirth
is borne

Virtuality & ducky-flux twinkling sub-rosa asparagus
hailing peewees' multi-vitamin
churches of upcoming goody roars
& yawns imbibing thailand junkies
harpooned with a metaphor forklift
dashed upon shooting-stars golf-ball
& I'm hooked via a slice of rain
writing dick tracey all-purpose uselessness
knife-throw erupting glass-ceiling of income
deep-sea metamorphed angels floating licorice heebeegeebess
instant diamonds in your alluring tide
ufos winking foamy-phonemes
jailing bananas who hasn't gone
yeti dazzling each snowflake

necklace taloose-le trek
sweating crystal-balls
kneeling wildhood
just outside a handball-court..

Your personality ethics a pri ori
nada fortune mnemosyne
that, I'm running-down now before my origin
emptiness gives spaced-out quizzical info
whirling into granola ice-cream tip-offs
magic hankering acme nursing a factotum
idling, keeling ideas from thy curls' bellhop
waves nipping at our gunwales like a jaded tortoise of finland
ecology lie-detector kisses away headaches into smiling coast-
    lines
reading the dark oomph of my quiet brainstorm, ginsberg
    doing our crash-pad dishes
when she's heaven in kitchen-maids, ungrounded, feeling-
    space
inebriated breeze, ulotrichous daylight
recycling open to a gesturing musical tree
may limpidity be upon thy dusty paths
cameling wheat-gold hills
diamonds & graphite
breathing legionnaires
jilted above the cloudy-ramadan
blazing ecru, vexed railroad abstraction
happy blue stork out-stepping pygmalion quicksand
flying everywhichway without a station that's always home

Quintessing eventual awareness with the patience of harrie-
    carrie mother-courage
a voice scattering lurky teens, old untold soul in new break-
    dancing jumpstart islands take-off flaming on his insect-
    bristling arm elbowed to church shaped like a telescope
immunity remix, counting kisses tarry infinite fingers at her

whippersnapper beanpole
inter alien ecola olamic with a fuse to your news, what's a
musefuck, ghosting slips
the chattering of adding-machines view thru a neutral ice-
cube white-giddyup of frozen opium diaphanous minerals
hallucinating emptiness upon their skinny limericks merry
ownership pass all feel-rays nonsense death wailing an
echo in a jug of grail, raining inkadew chimes in a rickshaw
shaving to play whittling twiddler-thumbs, loyal as a
butterfly, alight to venture thy night-tide & hedonic-signs
uturning overalls thunderous-covers doupleganger agent
waving breath lives in mystic reflections, duuzy heroin
looking before their opium earth shadows chess-moves on
the weegee planchet misspelling gramarically
abacus dingleberry black freckles unnameable nameless
sysaphus hand in hand
laced enlightened virtuality teeming with metaphyics
fibbermagee of peek-a-boos
if edolins on the haunt of adjectives crash thru your baby-teeth
graveyards virgin membrane
pneumonia catipults a star in my lungs, that if it grows over
incarnation is not extinct
will be my flying philosophy sans one cross-bone-flag justice
beyond vitalism?
icorus riding on this kickapoo curly-ques new-glue in a snuff-
flick-reality out-of-control
gerrymandering ions zugzwang bossanova escaping diamond
adrift miner's cap & a torch of bright dais-lies of the oracle
vampiring pollyfeemus third-eye hooded-zygote-badge
wrestling vitamin's nightmare in guess-why's leaping
zombies' kiddycart
banging om upon random grand yummy impractical intuitional
picadilly
soatting up the multi-universe crowned by eucaliptis stars
who don't know whose they are in their next rich moment
cradled bye-bye rocking grin pendulum following inside
laws just vanishing purple cauliflower untouchable drama
flashing most at rest kin-aggrading lift off the beginning's

greek swan-dive, info-action voltaire thoughts cliff-noting
  wit's own brink rinky-dinkum spinning, wheeling, galaxies'
  mind on pilot-light alert
protestors in an envelop vibe from othering defined a
  grip listening key-holes run-out like ankhs wooing the
  gingerbread mail, keeping the bills that stick to the ceiling's
  peanut butter tin-cup donald-duck living off of uncle-scooge
  dipsticking the middle-east
entombed in dunes whispering morse-code cream-cheese
  gambling dawn
thru foxy kindling reverse turban masks bundle switch-clicks
  neutral is, differing up perfect categories virtual yet real
  legend edgewise out-bounds, index in the ear of a teacup
  neptune recording angel-dust muse up-side-down rising
  illusions steam-shovel
underground wendle homes bethshheeba katabatic nuns
  scotta
this is a jigsaw-puzzle with all its embryos

Crazy-gluing a sphinx of nosegays horse-shoeing jardinière
whistling 'til I'm puckered-out, repeating what may lonly be
  once
ferns before dinosaurs built skeleton-key atolls humpback
  tulips
pimpling cap-size beheading lava valentines jiving your
  ancestral suicide bunkmate
unspoken kerplunking esoteric monkey-wrench root-a-ma-
  toots seedpod parachute
jujitsu arithmetic tumbling up the quasars' pseudopodium
  caught in website veils
newspaper enraptured fireflies torching unknown darkness
it could be a gila-monster with the measles isled in the sky
  around us
beyond its reticular arrows of parmenides' deluzeian elbow,
  checking a kickoff
vegi-nerves, gia shitaki interferon wing-ding duckbills hanging-
  on yin-yang

pegasis seesaw along within grains of radium ley-lines
    inclusive agapé bell-dive
middleweight yeats hammering stagecoach's orangutan woke-
    up dawn interviewing outer-space auswitz tricky betwixt
    extinct reincarnations' limbo, gently side-stepping
rim-jobs abyss trekking perimeters of dreamtime infinitesimals
    worshiping a baby-skull
chalking, drifting away from its ebony, hip to the opaque
    gospel buzzword network
wild skinflint kindergarten allah rye ennui

Banana pajamas don't turn-over your ale, gertrude stein
instant ritual-rebelling anti-conjective figuring dewdrops
mirror-genie camus on a j-curve
inebriated by the nirvana of heaven's split infinitive
multiplicity acquisitions wild crab-apples valleyho
ramose flux steelhead nerve benumbed toothfairy
    embattlements
dawn, moon sweat cascading endlessly before
adaptive evolution intuitive nonsense jumping abstracts
hemlock leopards intelligent whim
productive free-slaves of unlimited ergs
improvising libertads
creative sorcery with the lettuce to get-out-of-jail
kitty-tongue woo-brail, decaffeinated alpha, uncle humps

Nanos valaoritis
only the restless are trapped by a mime
signs over here
gone fawn view
tip-toeing with pussyfoot
on this lotus eggshell headache
you don't clever lambkin, bunny-hop
near to the sight of a mystic watchtower
islands hymen daemon tide-pools
under-glass mastiffs zazen insectitude in a greek shadow-play

polis against the individual knotty in hermit's nautilus
to badiou we are new longer than a spark off guru mumblypeg
    code-breakers
high-climbing outa their lion-claw robot bathtubs, dripping
    with of grand mal enlightenment mercury onto steroids
    enshrouded racing hymn selves, differing every differing
    known not known bicameral in the circular myth
escaping letters phoneme wordplay into the body of language,
    road-kill track-meet
impavid upon highways graveyard powdered with ecru tailing
    moonlight
blanched to be invisible adrift just listening rainbows flow thru
    me
tickling australian diesels irish bagpipe in a cave of lucid
    osmosis windows
melting dali evenings franswaw villon hung before a question
    mark
sailed in this cast of paleface bob hope in a noh drama
god tells them that only the oddballs can show-up
then jellybean mystery potato-race itemized amuse
dreaming lungs
the imafgew of the herabouts
almost delightfully unknowable
nam day plumes brusing twilight
alias infant google numbers random knuckle
windmills in the pitchblende
sense-ground drumming up grounded cummerbunds
entitling only the restless to be immured by a mime-sign
over here an-fond you divine cage of grieving bicycles
origami tide of pearl-divers reincarnating jupiter in a hopscotch
novel futures jabbing useless misspelling desires
production-lineup
flash gorden your q
you will-be divining in a cage
open swinging goodbyes
indoors handballing with this abyss
life-coaching skakespeare in an everyway gyro-compass
treasure lyrical plain-speech

announced on my innersanctom
your dreaming ghost

Pernickery further blasting rock &-rolls out grammar school
    windows
in-between escaping the cradle moon-dwindled a little your
    reflection-spooky angels
iambic quiz thy wild hairy rabbet bebop bopeep eggy-bootlick
    drift-swift in my twilight awaking dawn, I'm scrambled in
    gold-rays
universes' nova in my eyebrows flying way-away
get-a-way with the theory of always blazing across meme
    dreams
in yes-screen syneasthesias what's my line, now just rakes off
skinny veils available for questioning by anyone's crazy-quilt
    kindergarten
universal flash gensing lighting up on narrow-arrow
kneeling cherry-picker sparing with a baboon
fill in here with the birdy krishnas that sing along
cling on plankton trolleycars, bellhop into a mirror
that gets cloude- up with your breath
finding you alive reading you your left-rights
the novelling wet-finger unlimited
getting flashbacks virtuality I'm playing in my imagination
stagecoach babies crash-pad landing upon homeruns dusty on
    a funny-farm
cundalinni kangeroo-rat slippery within the bathtub flipped by
    your haystack
dingdong inducting conductors wandering out of their usual
    minds
ice-storm pompadour grip a cricket on a peanut these words
    I'm swearing in yummyfun in a mad-bible to what happened
    to the little gentle rain that fell from heaven? Or am I
    pondering on some weird acid trip? glancing new-myths
    thru Jell-O straws oaring maelstroms quivering lethe auras
    brain-stumping wholistic intellect down-front pharaohs
    rowboat skatebug many ee-cumings in your go-cart digging

to breathe neo-stoics luv dumb slime tugboat yugas,
blackout, that cricket on a peanut needling in to useless art
may tease your jockeys, or a republic caught flatfooted virtual
   ubiks
moot remote mute bliss socks knitting so-so complicated
   jimmy-jewfree
who that never grew into zen-chops only think-blank alias his
   creative personas
or is this worlds playing marble-comic-scripts antimatter
   go-gaming neo-shakespearean thermometers' asterisk
   heavens in the fallen gate, wiffenpoofs the unfelt velvet
   letter roostering prouse, alliteration's grouse, dark & tans in
   your fay-gay shadow origins of any faintly ancient uneasy
   odets-oday-o up-late evening with roaring night listening
   for thy knocking rattle storm-troupers guarding the doors
   of meteoric galaxies, wounded, raspberry swoon on your
   lips, I'm the crimes of industrial-diamonds, the rare seeking
   the unknown press a kid of balaneses wakeups, minus
   the giant alarm-clock detectives pawning zugzwang nova
   enzymes traveling via that's buggy folk-disease, quick
   lateral, meditate, pillbox, shut-up humming ventrioquee
   origami gymnastics enfolding infinitude metaphors no
   jailhouse plutonium too unbroken to breakfast different
   differing vodka-spirit mineralling one nuclear-yankee indian
   everything goes when your looking for heat standing atop
   grate
fallen under me chaos scales waiting for their heavy-weight
   no-doze
the stadium wild-funk reaching juice pioneers of the
   netherworld
index uplifting a breeze mumbling wheels on the real
   ganymede
smack-dab, limerick, rickshaw, nod

Shilly-shallowing along for a dive off the endless leap
network with daggers of bird-land ketchup you yuppy radical
   of luv
sliding questions ubiquity doesn't know where to alphabetize

these breakout axioms from hokey-pokey name, languid
  ghettos
hanging about dancing shadows on blue corners or limousines
  in the rain
dropkick sidewalks of porky-pig investigate exclusive wild glue
crowded among this funny madness turning into laughing
  hope
guide-wire science idealizing unique iterations kiddy-cart prey
  raids if you
kung-fu info, wuu-how & bisque attention quivers, don't fall-
  over my jumping-beans
already crashed the giants there's more than one you know
no-self quotes again we don't exist we just insist, reverse this

DUMBSTRUCK & SLAPHAPPY
Be quicker than a memory glance
opening a page of toasty dreams
economies dying & reborn
new-math inner-plays coming in numberless presage
bringing out groups of irish setters in their wigwag
distant intuition without geometry
where everything's tripping over itself
switcherooed in confused enlightenment
hypnotizing robots alive for your beginning nothing
lassoing a fishnet of kind sky's instinct
numbskull channels vortexing a kaleidoscope of hindu-hells
or lickety-spliting your barbecue mindful
have you been whiffed by a turtledove fire-escape lately?
numened great gatsby in a dandelion ?
thumbing fantasy muses
archetyping unique peeps
young & dumb enough to be mistaken for one
knobby radio-vibe blitzkriegs within you
heart-attacks looking for their valentine
lazarus rose-garden killing every gone-forever-return
flyweight monkey-shining jaded-shade
landing on your mental sandwich?

bo-peep unique yin-yang panda-bear moonlight
notre-dames grasshoppering upon your eerie drumstick
marble newspapers listening to a swimming pool of electric
    chairs' waterfall
hiccup galloping thrown jump
drinking from a line of you-who
flipped out somersault prop-job
taxiing bodies thru jesus karma
reincarnation ascendant hang-gliding erecter-set
interpretive twerp wiring bugs bunny snowdrifts
my question is not to question a J-curve with a dot-com under it
my feelings distil space/time
congealed between your knocking-knees spelling-bee
vanilla-manila meltdown this quark-communism
hair-shirt scratch-pad gambling a knit-sweater of palm-trees
underwear nagasaki rocking within swing-low lantern's grim-
    reaper
just above my waving hayride
exuviate, scarp, gyre, teeter, précis
membrane osmosis fading to hide in the dim-light

ONIHR for inversion dali
speakeasy teething pillows
your jellyroll bib mistaken forgiven
or sui-generus dreams on the brink escaping a utopian prison
ojibway in an escape utopia open
karl popper ski-lifting feeling condensed-space
thumbing the humbug off peter-built life
camus with his solipsistic we
unknown my alone-clone open
latch-key sleeping with a question-mark
massage blues hewing upon chocolate train wrecks
my questions gather into harrie-carrie rickshaws
tarboosh flyswatter shell-game dismissive without an envelop
between my knees quintessence congealed in meltdown
quark communism gambling scratch-pad hair-shirt thunder
beneath a knit-sweater honey deserts' warm glow

underwear nagasaki's rocking in the swing-low pirate-lanterns
just above my waving hayrides your jellyroll bib scrolling
    curlicues
mistaken for swiss-cheese queer aquariums' third eye
    kaleidoscope
hiving quick ambering crazy-glue gravitons
raving jumbo-jets syneasthesias x-ray beany-cap
hammer up & down equations stitching grasshoppers
more like a zap of rivers invading cracks to become a kosmic-
    sponge
identity underneath wafted away by cheery fears no longer of
    patterns jag
lit-up our glass of novas blazing pathologies alaska kindle
    enameled charm

Prickly tapioca
qued numbskull
still on rewind?
cellphone-sundial
attention makes timelessness jump
guru crooked with a face-book on-straight?
deserts wrinkling from grief struck, breathe tightwad
herman hessee out-guessing the net of ubiquity
cyclotrons of weathercocks magnified catching a flame
when evening burns its dreams
I'm laughing tooth-fairies
my nights cradle the bow of a pitching graveyard
jail-hat visitors giving synecdoche
transcript all the new-worlds here
lip-synch dromedaries & baby reveries
gesture dancing untouchable nonsense
abstracts impossible intimacy
every day a muse is big news
perfect-bound finger-prints
thumbing galaxies
without a superior complex now
just bow-wows to alchemy's dip

senile vibes
traveling reporters
looking for a crazed frequency
mantras wuuing timid hymnals too
enshrouded as normal agnostic betweens
returning where mirrors weep
& kitchen-nooky spirit unions
reify in flesh taboo
to skip over this
napkins in handcuffs
digital freckles sawdusting jamaica
you haiku a racket of keepsake
while mercurial self takes on what's cutup
feathering paracelus beyond arithmetic
gay-rays past the rationality of strawberries' cock-sucker
there's imagination's blackhole, walky-talky
freeze-dried musicality
where numb brail drifts you
ascendantly hip to the nerve in one curve-ball
Instruct within
kicks, blows, a undying that won't do you completely in
matches to failed utopias
ignore sleep-cradles origin
habit language april march
ramose into fiddlesticks
engram deems at yo'all service leonardo da vinci
with miss ink-spots, gesturing arabian letter-
scarves,,, night-rides thru rainbow ghettos
crashed inside jucusee bathtub eddies around islands' flesh
dreams within soap-bubbles too zonked to pop thru
sheepskin elbows, off the table with your cheops
flip-flop vortex, read your own kung fu filibuster
keepsake scraps, gertrude stein, hippy dactyls
clan began against huh carpetbaggers' vampire badminton
reverse fear onto itself shuttlecock decapitated ideologies
underground touch blazing gentle as crude inventions
     jewelling wing-dings
face before origin sikhs its template phantom breathing limbo

even anti-entropy
abyss break-dancing upon non-dimensional fuzzy wiggles
distinct & clear
modal-wishes teasing a launching–pad
goofus caressing sun-up
yawning lions in a freckle
wrecked ocean hums blue-fur
risky quiet infrequent probability
average declaratives hidden in the noble lay-abouts
iceberg busted
miming socrates
tap-dancing bottom-line aristocrates entangled
frankenstein's rockinghorse chair
grinning in the attic of tattle-tale wind
scumbling brush-off-diamonds
don't fetch quizzical tizzy
I'm sailing with rd lang
cruising tom-toms
to beat an ezra pound
law ruled by wild sui-generis jinni
alive via osmosis dharma hugs
curve, grip, pool-rung
emerge with your lungs
abreast puffed up together
justice rage emblazed in a campfire
ghost waves the yellow flames
reincarnated in-betwixt each breath
in & out thru a crazy void
micky-fin in a bout with knock-out–drops
escape what always is
galvanic proost humidity
slipping into unknown deeds, find opening brew
act voltaire wells-fargo radar smiles
more empathy than apex's gorilla toothpaste
distance lost in abstractions' intimacy
compelled quarks radical fate
bliss awareness novas exact returns
many platypus canoes guide indonesia

tar-feathered wing-nut, upright maple-leaf
spin-rad at once to the lab of bantam hens' think-tank
where philosophical roars
debate metatrainean toenails' wink
dipping into quivering lethe, open, scripted
 thrown feeling reflections' big-bang vase
smithereened every dream-moment
we all have a kosmic part glimmering within
teeder-tottering our jigsaw
embryos shanghied in a winkum-blinkum & nod container-
    ship
glee jumping aboard ergs trigger heat-senses pheromes'
    mumu
walspurgus blazing dark-matter's invisible gravity reversed
meditating with hermeneutics vibra-harp kvetch
lovely head thrown akimbo grinning wuu boats
oared by mullah nasrudin track-meets flying no-means of
    support
illuminati disasters woodpecker looking hummingbird
    optometrist
cyclops of my third-eye one free intelligence innumerable
    minds
dizzy stones in a river-bed, inhibitory nervous-system hip in
    fast currant
winnowing dead-ends raying from my gemini jeweled derby
    magic
encapsulated technology? I'm breathing water-wheels,
    liquidity alive

Amuse ripping entitlements
until he came within a quarter shebang
whose every co-sign & voice
gave impersonating perhaps here-to-now
will rogering feelings balance
isek denasin oysters & champagne
whatever gets you on to that's all folks
quantum space-puzzle measured yet what's in it

funny-bone enigmas? vibe glance claws pause
hammering like a billygoat across a maori fence
limbs as big as geiger-counter torso slapsticking herds of
   unheard drums
felines with buffalo thunder, mind-neutered libertarians
raying around for cues-&-clues, while probabilities of the
   impossible
this existence, ahah! hipnopalmic flight in-betwixt guesses
   truth & a soul diner
ride your phantom jinx ovary thing is recorded in the akashic
   vibe except stem-cells
listening nowhere jumps, hip-hopping kangarooing quaaludes
   hongcong cafeteria rainbows
families blazing ketchup jazz, any bodies stiff ding-donging a
   false liberty bellhop of chocolate pets? brain-damage taking
   over robotics modeling kinetics greet the ungifted
hiding in their skinny newsprint, wino question marks rooted
   in India
dishwasher buddha la omnibus playing with fingernails
your attention have I laid-back when egg-ship ovalteened in
temple painful cries stilled in marble hallucinations
unheard absurd birthing a merry-go-round
which never returns to itself
nude habits unique enough to be shot at though not hit
get-loose questions whiz brew up your creation
remember no-engines in alpha digital toolybush
instantaneous zap over speed blurs into waif-mirrors
dada-ma at the funny-farm discovered paw was queer for all
before odd-fellows lifted earth-wise
christmas polterqiest shooting-stars
raindrops moonlight greek ivory invisible oxygen again

Hunkered down underground
listening to coltrane
sauntering thru iridescent raven mister big
kaleidoscope villanelles
quivering hairdos, glee traffic fugue in jiving-jams

off battle smiles, labyrinthine ideologies' un-marker
time-games frame virtual origami jacking rubik-cubes
adventure cosmic geology, metaphysical pragmatism
within olamic ubiquity, vagina hemlock camouflage revelation
irish dark toothless verity, molasses lawnmower equals away
bi-location wave-particles split honey of aubade
diving in my crash-pad feeling sleep bounce
awake literalist dinosaurs remodeling ice-pick tap-dance
climbing occipital maelstroms of venus flytraps
dissolving letters unto the ink of a drunken anthill cakewalk
gurus envision, deep in-every persona you avail
hearings written to miss blank crop-circles fingerprint tattoo vortex
alien mazes networks jellyfish parasols diaphanous swimming
    reflections
numb immunology until el-ghazali whirls in a ulotochous pun,
    cleverly wise
fuck alliterative troglodytes, hunkered down above the skyward
puddling-huddles imploding tied up in a singular flip-flop prop-job
birthing wing-ding buzzards until clitoris doorknobs paul revere
bugged via feedbacks of elfin hymns
imaging jinni machines kinetic freedom
dream insomniac riches in your life
just enough for this beyond goody-gumdrops
spinning you into a naughty knot
escape juggling rainbows' hot-ice

Open glee
wave-length sailors bellybuttoned alian curly-q
I'm formation rules whiz the love-peace-sign
giving you duo index-finger before hello
does your gun have an impulse
like zeuses double-thunderbolt
quantum-loop-gravity inquiry
dianetics rig-vata novocain
extreme counter-revolutions spinrad into a hum
pinky underneath the ghost of art
whisper misspelling nonsense

impossibilities dredged up like sunrise
curtailing flocks of belief
the smuu we live upon
yonder in our ivory enlightenment
with computorised toothfairy pillowfights
no need of a quill
Sans any bugle-call , un-occupy-able
hammock under fireflies mingling nova oddball
kiddies in the goof off quiz-idea tax inheritance
many lines in this container-ship
headstrong
   diamond
       echoes psyche
       kneeling
 nymph, finish me
clamoring wet-walls
tittily inkling breezy mist
are our you U dismembering
never-gone
        jungle-gyms'
pickle-barrel

of   (write your you're rite right left ovarian here)

     uranium fish miniaturized unto elementals
         rainbow dyed jive with scrub-brush confessions
hermeneutic lucidity abyss vacating nada
      total-rebellion
         drinking emptiness
            freckled wheat in cyclops moonlight
unknown anonymity
            lamming upon shuteye
               funny-farms' blue
    electric habit

Flying asleep upon within
ken declarative boomerangs
weaving a cats-cradle slingshot
feeling up normal group theories
riots in midnight breakfast
spidering armies worshiping rice
concrete templates
giving hotfoot idea
tiddleee winking jacks
acquisitive digging hip-hop gunnysacks
iambic pentameter upside-down trance
quasar well-knowns flaming by
unsettled home always
plaurism dancing wicky flux
mongoosing the cobra-question
listen tattletail reeeds
zazen crashed inside
automatic orangetang
retired brake-job
horny vampire
zillion suits
quick as a psychopath
hindu tobacco fillered thru john rawls
goodygumdrops big mind within this little one
every science draw phazmagorical
mystic betwixt any tock of your clock
slow-time in quick lanes for this birdseye
liberty frozen veggies, the oven of luv
presaged whiffs of jigsawpuzzls
at peace with their embryos'
umbilical super-string hand-puppet
go-along concatenations reified bilateral vibe
parachutes in the starting-guns of daisies
landing upon a meadow of wooden-nickles
jumping my breath like crazyhorse
impulse rhythming equal abstractions
perfect circle each hoofer whiffenpooph
beyond the outer airy farrie making twilight this unique queer

unseen via third-degrees, hip jade
shape-shifts over invisible flesh
cradling myth
swim, beginning
never again
haunted eardrums'
immortal gesture
memeing to pachyderm
hebrew greek italized french vergs
dishwashing lapidary joys upon gee
windy tears, inventing your radar
acashic davy-jones lear–jet kind geniuses
cat-walks on a tightrope rainbow spider-webfoot
numinous hymnal balance upon quizzy saucers deem
galaxy merry-go-rounds climb within inner-timeout
distill your quintessence in the holy grail of universal braille
spun finger vaz
enigma puzzle
levels
your catch-up question behind an exclamation mark
homeruns' knockout-drop
vanishing under a cherry-tree.
known only a little by earth
since we haven't landed for all imaginations' membrane

Hypnotized alive
the earth stands up
liquid black flames in your mirror
reverse physiognomy nom de plume
inundates your cell just what it deeds
inheritance taxidermy, private eye of all
golfing mothballs up-against sisyphus dung-beetles
nova fanatics misspelling the uncaused cause
listening here-abouts artificial whale tail-fins
speak to yird, erase your golem forehead lines
imprint dishwasher memes
wrinkled beyond translation like the brain

small enough for you to know & unknow
mystic dungeon, tear kung fu wise syllables
thy nerves have too many polarities
2 decide with one.

Know the dim between
yird echoes in leprechauns of jade
virgin salt dashed away
by quick pacific tongues
& checker-box butterflies
glancing off my shoulder-blades
twin wing-seed reincarnated genealogies
heavy daemons lacing up my nervous trolley car
pronking out your surfboard flash gorden appears chipped,
    teething
shark-gene, operative, eternally reincarnated for who-izt
of no kind, tribe-vibe, escaping with ultra-altruism blasting off
    the stardom-pad
nova festooned kinetic validity
upside-down giant iridium
at the skirt of curtains
fine-combing mushcrat reflection
gesturing past duckbill whipping cream
it's our intricate untouchable two-shay olay
pinned up holy grinning from your click
elemental wheeling rickshaw lightfoot
jumping upon skippydos overhead alabama gemstones
making novelties unique
interlude enter bio-friendly creative project
not rare virgins in cellophane
jelly-rolled up sashay diplomas
top-knotted pincushion chopsticks acupuncture
quills on needles & needles on quills
tripling fingerprints coil-spring detective amanuensis
jagged winter-peek-a-boos
dnaed with frankensteins
afloat upon the air

iceberg breakout
zombies' rhubarb
blood-lines seeking unrecognizable's original pre-birth
    character excuse
wrestling jungle-gym intimate abstractions, licorice at a taffy-
    pull
retired off looking at you in kiddy-cart wishing-wells' distilled
    image
even though dreaming neon-time forever-gone anywhere
is only thy cushy virtue within missions' haze
lifted from rimbaud's drunken-boat
inkadu snapdragon, unbuttoning pop-cycles
riddled enigmas baked opaque
& the teenage phantom of your one-legged corpse
erects with a sigh

Jawbreaker marbles
taking out & viewing his eyeballs
aligned upon freeze
sculptors riding
hiccups bedspring
probabilities tracker
curves that adhere
& instantly escape
quantum gaps
space to write
around me
lariat cocoons
supervient emergcies' hummababi
just niched enough not to be a drive-bye

Head of swamps
chased by theologians' dung-beetle psyche
then mind echoes
living battles
co-evil peace

via the inner reflections
winking blindside
nada surrounds
tautologies' rebellious inhibition
saddled upon a laughing giraffe
edgewise-info wrestling kung fu top-see-turvy
returned upon a spin character narrative
imprinted liquidity hum down to quick freedom
incoming upon the catch-me-blues ziggurat mumbo-jumbo
salt & peppering my pok a-dots, avalanche ratiocination
knells tollgate, wizard sans gelled image
reading vibe-currents
fuzzywuzzy up-faced lucid-blur now
ghosting by with super-nova crash-pad of the day
darting zombies, frankenstein's aphrodisiac
technos queer for thy middle-road spinal-column
hilarious grand peanut-brittle ice-pond yes, but
omni-directions slipped into the lemon-aid parade
encoded haunts whizzing by your invisible tracks
in-between guillotine tiger-eyes & the rainbow knighthood
meandering around a loomis-truck
dizzy wheeling relax slide-rule
even if buddha probabilities
cradling your hold-up
rein in brainy membranes
gallop your tick-tock away here
exchanged for the beat within you
zilch flying niches, opening squeeze-play
instamatic flash, vibe-tribes
brushing off rough-diamonds
sea-shell whispering digital
quantum boxcar eternity
rattling clicks without no soul-mate
then via planned chance
twin infinities entwine
one abstractly detached
my ubu bellybutton
like your churning milkshake

tumbling around our fall walks
jabber-walking philosophy
laughing dance-floors of the undefeated nobody

Infinitely divisible until
krishna cash-registers
bell-hopped into feeling
auras' halo
maroon tunes
lackadaisical ease
leaping a shape-shift of calculus
arcing under numbskulls' glass-ceiling
herculean fantasy withholding open the jaws of yawn beyond
dualistic ping-pong tripping over its net metabolism
super-woman clocking her wristwatch
original bangles ringing their etheric flesh
phantoms of akimbo nullifying each lull
ganymedes curled in deeds
threading prophetic riffs
happy mousgateer gambling `nightfall
when the club of spades is quietude asleep

Rare schools
minus know-it-all indifference
outrun the loner of wave-length zap
breezing tickles
leaping onto my wheel
yodeling radio
tattle-tale jingles with skeleton-keys
yet no closet
where raga paintings
beginning vibe foundation
opening ubiquitous always
thru skitzies' jitterbug
peeping out of your lucky fugue
adolescent elephantine ganesh
pregnant cloudbanks

bumping off a rubout lightening-tree
nom de plumed
as f. scott Fitzgerald insignia
daggered in the high wind
sleighing with mind on electron jumps
cyclotron warm-up, ambling in to pitch
geometries of tiddleewinks mandala
irregular clues rational labeling upon embryo jumping-beans
avoiding beany-cap prop job skeleton-crew
night-time jumbo-jet in a holy nosedive
engram frame-ups gene-pool
organizes with more than gin & tonic hiccup westerns
sprigged by mint & cut-of lime.
or finygunswake wolfing huckleberries dingdong apocalypse
held together light unzipping our aura, kissed love-bites
cabal tribes attempting to pen & torture me for my difference
'weez been too many eons living in your unconscious brahma'
caught meditating lumber-mills chimed in with their seesaw
disguises of why birth hit thy rocky-road gumshoeing your
      teeth alum
snapshots on crutches pointing to euclid
ladders into old measured feeling
qua-being unforgotten ancient nows

Dillydally whirled in,
I'm for long space/time flip
condensed ideograms tangoed
whims drifted into galloping heaps
blinking rainbows flashed from weathered barns
eternity never coming back to itself au fond
feelings dissed in alien look-a-likes
tears swam upon mirages' jelloed protoplasm
galaxy hysteria charaded around in a mathematical headdress
science entwined with imaginary operations, teething bamboo
lucid memes haloing distilled vivariums
tailoring your phantom fit
aura overcoats withdrawal

unsnap every shoulder-holster heart
lift out the peacemaker's quantum rocket-ship
metaphor july & warp to nowhere known.

Myth verses fantasy
I'm playing worlds
random scattered
then drawn into a grip of all-hands
that open flaming
differential equations
gesturing time/space
asleep ye wake unconscious
in a forest of blue fir
tickled via needles
glowing from the lap
& nook of overheard absurdity
crystal mills' transparent
guiding little diaphanous
to null responsible denial
switcheru witchcraft
adversary buzz
swinging down
new tailored inside
fylfot leaps up
vibe wave
truth running into puzzle
miss of thy cycles
veering on-track
empty of blankety-blank
live ammo in rubber-band pigtails

Critique return
aslant vectoring
gulps kissing wavelets hello goodbye
lifting by an evolutionary wristwatch
dangling fingers

gesturing talkies
metaphysical daisy off summer haze

Quilled down launches umpteen robots
lined around their blocks in a fathom's hug
inside dreaming memes conversed gertrude stein-wise
oaring skeleton link-ups
flapping naps of rhythm
chewing the goose-bumps
shouting across metabolism
whispers disguised in a husky voice

Wresting topology, climbing the surface bell-curves
microscopic industries your turf's the epiderm
inventions wild quick death-march & april shopenhouer
janus of gemini
nom de plume fluttering in your cat-door
attracting smithereens
tweaking eeks
village unto bonbons
fuzzy mystic stopwatches
crystal-balling dew-drops
hollogramed acashic indra
waving to meta-mind
you step in easy breeze
thinking limbo monkey-wrench
winnowing alembics
spelunking otherness
not wanting to be eaten in plato's allegorical cave
unforgotten birth
with so many conceptual entanglements

Unconscious flying carpets
ready-made warhol airports
I'm a garuda hip-hop

virgin chair
dancing ice-cream fountains
edgewise pineapple
caressing thieves' light-touch
whittling stardust ferryboats
upon a raft of hurricane opinions
sweeping up your breathy muse

Rumble skinny
nibbling eraser
unless day fact reversed
with avatars'
eternal oddball
multifaceted being
always split

Elastic giddy-up
out of it & ride
everything is different already
quintessences that ken such othering phenomena
biological adam into evening flux
winnowing random alembics' continuum
guided via mathematical being-hood
the real in the imaginary with or without the imaginary
quantum blank personas unto the infinity division of
    subatomic minuscule
entity identity zombie structures yet alive at the base
complexities arise signal verisimilitudes private games
diatom of understanding light up thy empty wise jellyfish
kosmic nervous systems vibing funny/farms
to peruse writ large emotions
ballerina heart'simpulse
diaphanous jellyfish gymnastics
nooisphere upon tiptoe
alien bias oddball immunity
never so turned around

you encompass your multiple-self
dislodging thy quark of creative jumps
just faraway as you pioneer here

Wishing-well
germane jailbreak
u-turning into your dappling canoe of smiles
& a bucket of hiccups
encrypted deciphers
if chance
subatomic upstart
warming up the dwarfs
minerals hi-signing proteins
in islamic getaways
rainbow flames of heaven
blazing a page of truth
illusions of vishnu
reified in structures of luck
wheeling, commingling
almost twins
each othering
tripodal swing
forever yemen me beyond
gong dingdong's wing-ding
withdraw ye u
into the rickshaw tent-show
nuclear break-dance
spin the holy grail
it was passed around until I passed out the exit
complexities unkenned thru origins' rebirth-speed
idle down to your slow jiving coocoo-clock
bowling alley vichyssoise
flying mother-goose
tricksters lickity-split
questioning hangman ironing-boards
tongue-job flying-carpets
walking the planks of ah

sirens oraculing earth-life
pool of remembrance.
membering new vacuities
open spaces of creation
random attention
totally wigwamed
super-duper-lazy
ease into the hip/hap
its just more difficult to be nixed by a meteorite
when your swiss-cheese binoculars
are melting in your vegan pork-chops
   & nobody's indian t'was iceberg-climbing upon lightening
   bolts
open & give cleverly to haunts of in-action
take roman-candles to breathless echoes

Determined happenstance
rorschach silhouette
many-colored yarns zap me
archetyped via mandalaing events
being-qua-being
qua-being-being
stirrup tricks
intentional chance
random quiddity
encircled, goodbye yuga auras of understanding
winter's rosebud
hearing tin-cup
mercurial saturn
awakening nod
engraming haywired dawn
wonder question your maze
find an ever-changing name
then pronounce it unfounded
because highflying ideas thou/thou
zoom quantum weeping-willow
microscopic bathtubs

just foaming surf
freebee cagey
or screaming whisper
colitis thru thy barcode
lizard digitals
hash marks' vector
panting after flags' opinion
curled up into the starting-gun
re-emerging unto osmosis abyss

Quantum hopscotch
softly always never without a span
passing osmotic
thru emotional caves
roaring in the gush
lucid, deem
tidy march-hares
bowling pin-drops
a sparrow owning thy gas station
fetal shmoo
united guillotine
distinguished virgil
sage lost in haywire
rational flight-plan dali motel
intricate growing wild pathways
climber aboard this laughing train-stop
dialing halos, retailoring auras
veils disguised as flaming membranes
urchin warlocks battling childhood orphans
squealing on nada untaken mystic left-alone
wheeling beyond hickory-dickory rundowns
a pitch of tears betwixt wig & nest
kneeling lightening-bolts' origami
law in the hiss of pencils
mercury rolling up their jailhouse
speakeasy timber-wolf dialogs
quivers of physics, eternal arrows off illusionary loadstones

guiding our dust-clouds reified wonderful quiz-kid universe
shape-shifting quicker than zulu photon's ganglia
decoding the absolute orchestra
escape in weightless love-teams
here, diving into clarity vacuum

Learning the prescribed rules for you to escape
because as you page repairs
inborn & acquired originality alienates you
to lengthen & disappearing in thy self-mirage
when there's ill-at-ease on all metaphors
your span of existence leftover goof-tracks
that will never be cured of happiness
follow doubt, kiddy-cart into nagasaki
everyone bicycles precisely
daredevil wild socialism for the young & individual laws
heretofore the untold naughty quotes
buying up my cells
sailboat your gravity-wave
poltergeist, roller-rinking upon our silver-heeled mercury dime
unoriginal kindergarten's veracious make-believers
reversed in this antique urchin
twiddled apart before the news
meta-narratived into fear
came fearlessness
bonfiring a greek of the sunday-punch
Burglar peaches
quick-tan race-card
akimbo yet I'm not whiffenproof
unspoke from his bike
envelops saddled in a rainbow
anarchist playing group-theory
yeoman who begins married to a forest
inviting the shadow of hanging- rock
appears olfactory as jungle gym
night rises in from the fallen mist
2nd guessing tunes religion like afterthought

quiet in the church of now? hummingbird dreams
beyond machine yet occipitals at the punchbowl
lion shaman nail gothic witch electron life to birth
catherine wheels radioscopic psychedelics
dusting butterfly's numinous wave
a spiny-urchin juggling in our hands
distant immunology calculated by vibe
geminis queer for each-other
umpteen together yet never the same
oregon-coast dawns a rusty-bucket
civilizations who blink in the split-log of lightening-bugs
along the quiver ganglia
interrupted by via bird-flutter
thundering my sunny window-pane
x-crossing back & forth this dollied heart of nietzsche
plato's church-mouse under my palm
whispering I'm not red riding hood's nottingham
I speak from above the ceiling overhead
I'm gnawing way-off-the-grid, electric, intimate, delight

When only singular virgins'
virgin frees an ultimate he-she
will gulliver tune-up
to musical arrows' super-string-section
deep incognito fabulist
precise enough to know when to keep his mouth at a zipper
to hear creation listening
ironical pragmatism
rake the fishing hockey
outa your briefcase ef8724lz
coletrain muse imagining
spelunker under-earth
nuclear-nuts unglued
internet exterminators
whittling brain prunes
mistaken for a fig-tree
your personalities jack-knife

tiny antinomies without quacking up
like pegasus smithy
mainline carriers duck-tailed
roanoke gambling file-cabinet neon
turquoise verses oxygen-masquerade
disguised in psychic unicycles
ego wheels under the big ah
you sweat so much your aquariums
in a swimingpool go-witness the wetness
frosted candy-apples dragon lava
miner's cap luna bending-to a poltergeist hail-storm
greenstone fiddling under department stores
ley-lines on the path of repeat
with a viola of yellow spines
made from kafka's cockroach
lightened by a zilling of infinite dawns
golding over with rose-petals of sunset arisen
rays breathe crazy-gluons
wound into india's takeoff
aristotle, this is a virtual-mix-up
of rorschachs lost in their shadow
haptic mind above this flesh
big wheels for me, tornados aura pin-drop
on celestial roller-skates upon the brim of saturn
haunches gitty-up children in the window flash
already dizzy from barber poles unicorn?
sign here & be visited by aliens of understanding
just before they get their merit-badges

Forever between & never out
except sleeping by dreams
weird lonely multiplies
& abnormal escapes
the grid-iron hut
begins to play
with something other than
who she thought this elf was

a mcgregor lumber-man
on hardboiled breakfast
estranging the alien of yourself into the real unique
you breakup into familiar othering
impersonators appear, clones of qualia
reassured web-foots platypus in on their duckbills
high-brow levels at elevator feeling
sexy as a green-hornet
dante-car open-mouth rumble-seat
political hypotenuse
strangling equations
bouts about fatima
may I lamm this with
no time to search for remembrance's
interrupted plenitude
bicycling on a giant eyeball
developed in a teardrop
upon thy snorkel
easy breeze walk
image symbol the real unsayible
is this another other of the other
hip behind my elbow?
airplanes of metaphysics
hailing liquid windows
integrity fear open
names disappearing into awareness
screaming echoic cradles
immunology turns to mad juice-bars
returning through abysses of our influence
nausea voids empty yet jostling within thee
you feel chaotic like a walnut bigger than
your douser vibrations veering off track here
attentive lineups escaping gertrude stein
cloudbank diagrams y'all
spin-rad, break-dance
wild, monotonous tweedly-dee

Picasso Communism
anarchist union
rice bowling a tic-tac
ulta-transcendental launching-pads
squirrelly at the gas-station
nuts in their virgin-pressed olive uniforms
camouflaging leprechauns' heist
immanence in-between there's emptiness & aries lair
icebergs of justice
a deck above medusa's jungle
open shirt-hairs conducting the breeze
unconscious diplomas enveloped by miscellaneous infinitude
nirvana says hello underneath your birth
chicken-little dancing on a low-fire grill
jumps into the big-dipper with a super-string of orgasmic
    puppets
battlefields of gladiolas worm-holing every time-warp here
armies at the end of my paint-brush
rush gesturing tumbles upon stampede
confusing enlightenment
nemesis matchbook
lantern behind a flame
orangutans, lackadaisical, sunset
wakeup evolutionary children of adaptive intelligence
quilted with ideology buttons nippling your ufos
psyche memes' funk
web-lint
virtual elite bleeps
delete delete
narcissistic cynicism
oh embryoed jumping-bean
rock within my gemstone
magnified damascenes of feeling
vibe-waves apocalyptic levels
rebirthing zizek bathtubs
claws griping earth
dirt-clods with black-holes' mousy tongue
german idealism elsewhere

jaybirds laundromat
ice-cream, coctoe

Anthropic-dragon sneezing
flying-carpets' handkerchief
initialed if/and/or/either/none
impossible twin curly-q
pigtail hokasigh duffy
with kirk's cuneiform
balls into a yoga
shooting-star
trading chalk
for its dust
yodeling nirvana chaos
higher than analog peek-a-boos
roaring from out of the universal ballpark
a cherry in a rose/parade of sundowns' dip
full of bleeding-heart kennedys
until valentines' arrive
& monarch hands flutter
in-between nocturnal bar-codes
& unaided gates open sesame's lamp .
dynamite rimbaud enslaved
flying nuclear calm
blind-spots abyss
education transformations
heidegger's ready-made something othering itself
puppeting chipmunk freeway
upon our golf-course slice of infinite pi
mathematically numbskulls
fausts with checkbooks
umbilliculed jiminey-crickets & the kit-fox muse
huddled untogether thundering random weathervanes
flying via goodbye beanycap wildly preferred
every dick & harry fur-coat more bald than nude-truth
river-rat alleys gatherer of orphan-wigs
erector-sets' underwear lotus eggshells

caressing gumshoe plankton resilience
diablo lipstick winking 'til sunrise
is a funny grin.
Mcluhan's radar
laughing puppeteer
a little scrambled
just the whites please egghead
keep tiny yellows for balancing the iron
black-eggs ancient like rainy night
delicacies in china now yugas ago
mothra everlasting under king-kong drums
sweating art tatem's frying-pan
lamming from diamond heart-strings
twirled by your witches' cradle
breathing myths
whisper thy horse-play
roaming among break-dances
one gray stone
I'm plowing thru Ivanhoe my childhood
startled without a beginning
voids nullifying inside set-theory
groping tribes babied upon their arachnid machine
hiving screen-doors rascal deeds
liberty stand, thought engram
dreaming peeps
meltdown awareness
neither the circle nor the line
evolutionary intelligence
coming back on itself like a will roger's lasso

Caterpillars fuzz in the smog of angel dust
mimetic receptive
I'm upon the bomb of my enemy
transcending acts of observation
living-rooms' subterranean pulchritude
broken from the release
spilt, wilding immense layaways

ping-pong galaxies
silhouette of daffy cream-cheese
little david playing on my heart
weird superb absurd inquiry curls fondling garden yard-bird
jailing braille along phonemes
voicing choices
rose petals lapping ember
spyglasses below hell
fumbling with my boneheaded voyage
thermostat metronome
dear genius 1920s with a buccaneer
crying sighs of osirus,
dodgy quivering river
engaged to merriment
canoes onward like two-headed arrows
pallbearing aluminum moons
stuck-up viking
distilled ear, please
quieted down to feeling again
noises into lullabies
kulturkampf over communist tide
where the spirits of underground are blooming
& only the dumbstruck unknow their knowledge
meat-boats plowing thru new antiques
detached & identified
from keeping wild earth
raying sufi baby teeth
always light inquiries makeup
jabs of parmenides
ushers of golfcourse justice
dharma wing-nut
scrotum figs & dionysus in a goatee
pipsqueak mountains alive vanity
caravansaries naked wiggle
trilogy upon the climbing-ropes of the harp
rapid dromedary curling quantum skulls
mirror-genes bubbling a gunnysack of fun
alliteration disappears in wits' mindfulness

transformed carriage off homeric penguins' webfoot leap

Dickybird race aced in the extreme
photographs guillotine necktie
mind camera flashing inside the sky off your head
goofs lighter than a kite-string
lets go of alien me
two rainbows
splitting honey-buns
enter my fairytale
nothing against just us
trickster kettledrum
humming stomachs
leapfrog upkeep
turn off the maddening computer
I'm afraid of vomiting on my radio
photon reeling in the unreal
flying without any between
galaxies overtaking every dish
front door enraptured
left a right-cross
xraying hidden tracks
impersonating yourself
unconscious nom de plumes
dizzy squeeze-plays that went akimbo
cake-layered mugworts & red handed
womb pirates escaping in a lead balloon.
david plumb
night views sunset embering
like giant antics upon a cantaloupe
swimm you merge with the orange light
quasars twinkle anton wilson x-crossing roy roger's bridge
fey with the eyes of a hip vampire tabasco pele
underground rivers mushroom loony waiting for dawn
philo, ero, nomos, agape, fugue, john henried by uppity ghettos
shacked-up with dreams & osmosis labyrinths' improbably
to escape the way-out games, receive the akashic

146

literal mass of dove-wings whisper thru their perfect-trade
  illegal laws
hived with yin-yang hyper-time insectitudes conductor of the
  nano ex-machine
lazanya flying theloneous monk upon william burroughs
  precise opium typewriter
awarms, ectoplasms' gumshoe lawn-mowing black-strap
  molasses
henry dave thoreau of the conical pencil whispering seths to
  the dali lamma
gurjieff ice-cream moustache & trapeesing spiderman
  algorithm, lightfold filigrees' inventive neuro-map,
  emblazoning yourselves hunched-down carmel fairytale
  leading science brain door opens ray cracks in like donald
  duck islam's wild mouse researching before forget-me-nots
  in love with huh enlightenment torch, reentering into the
  birth-apotheosis licking up your seaport road, DEEP FUN
  & HAPPY LIBERTY, PASSIVE NIHILISM SOLISTISTIC vade-
  meum AIR-WORLD mystic news everyday
planes landing down from the upper-ground patterns to
  hopscotch

Too high on an infinite storybook? deconstruct your bashful
  roots
past-lives stutter-gush REFLECTING IRRATIONAL
 unmistakenly wild-strike every-godess deadheaded thugz
yeti no queerer than conflating that with this patty-cake
  flapjack
abstract hermanuetic defaming fundamentalisms ratcheting it
  up
gaugan stepping-stones tooth-fairy in abandoned pillbox
memories imagination imagining to remember nepenthe's
  inviting enzyme jitterbug
flood all-tied-up quivering like a pointalistic dagger just before
  it waves mummyied temple storms leap in their carry-a-
  ways upon smithereens' deem
fondled by hugs acting like a casket, uplifts go down you know

there's dumb lingo smart enough to scare you nowhere ain't
    flying their zazen blank
& no plato linking their hennypennies, ramadan energy fuels
    the missing avoidance
null scry templates gingerbread fractals wheel-barreling pure-
    cane village about–where heebeejees meme impregnated
    fuck ecology, the distant invisible wind a meadow-lark
    skeleton hanging by lotus-lily third-degree ali babba
    mineshaft lamp, hallucinating bibles geminni parable, fish
    in calculus rocking-chair blind within liquid mirrors, peeling
    see-thru your keepsake whim nouns converting them
    untoward verbs, little poontang canoes
li poing your yo-yo rainbow?
have-been elf mugged by a gnostic?
join the unique playful disunion adventure
enigma circuses, incognito nom de plumes
sailing by mountain-peak dairy queen white-tops
varnish the night slowly approaching like bella lagosee
hipnotizing the globe-trotters into icorus yuppies awake
    lumberyard
frankenstein reaching out for india sewing cupped hands unto
    butterflies alight
just before eraser track-teams whypted-out maybe/perhaps
I'm putting together unfamiliar's liberty
tasting monster brew cooking thy heart of runes
gliding into my elastic dusty sidekick mark
hearing kids aches me nut
artist tortured by politics in hypocritical drag
belly-laughs calligraphy stealing night-fall
mythological leaves blinking imagined window
to finger a love-note through the steam of your breath

Vahalah
you deem I gave over my keys, watch & billfold trinity,
    metaphoring cellular
apocalyptical higgs turn-on, turn-off rna gene
for being thrown-in like a walk-in parachute recovery stature?

questions dancing with human sunflowers entangle me like a
   quantum anchor
smiling like a beast underneath empiricism's robot sky too
   inert for quick whims
make a bell of your dungeon

Hidden by gestures cup-dipping swan-dive
yuggas wheeling into your mind of dawn ?
turn-on to normal intimacy
fundamental glee, I'm either here or I'm not here
stay away rimbaud's I am not I, okeydoky
if hearsay mouse peeks at everest's white-owl
its improbable he'll be totally strolling with his gambling self

Pure aliens must be unrecognizable
via spirit definition, for otherwise they would be in us
emerging unique well-knowns
yet nobody kens what's in us yet
why-not quintessence elemental jumping rainbow trout
discoursing subatomic in our veins
neutral pogo all the way up/down everywhichway
flux doesn't make act this scrim rebellion
it's hammered unto infrequent moans of breaking-ice
e-mailing lily of the lotus dally with me now ambiguity
   clueless
instrument of all ritual worshiped by habits don't ghetto either
news-boy subtext
roman tarot cards
understanding foreign humors
exhaling oracles
no not daffy-duck listening to the inanimate
the shy one withdrawn like a mystical volcano
blast-off into high underneath doiling curbside physics
when you yoyo under the grapevines of reasonable jungles
   youngster
desires idle-wild into seraphims enlightened heavy only

landing at this place
together swimming thru infinite membranes, distinction
our inherent reclusive glue
wet enough to be free of

We ezra pound upon little-big grand bounce
lines of imaginary math
universes cherry-picked
vacuum-packed recursive
folded warps encompassed
mindful blood-bank jesus
appearing with vampire grail
drunk fingers

I'm carving inhibitions unlimited beyond thought
asparagus-tips never know themselves to well
hegelian parachuters jelly-rolled
emerald drop-fingered across catholic keys
rationality handcuffed to science
a brewer of dust translating mediums
alpha-pragmatist kung fuing into gesture
baby-touch encapsulated via struggling crucibles
adaptive winnowing thru deep easy lifetimes
fashionable heredities along the cellular link-up
quantum economy minds hiding within the latest awareness
guru voodoo typecast fly-fishermen enflamed rainbows
conducting infinite bands wavy abreast
stranded on contingent arpeggios
winks popping from roiling kickapoo
varicose lava mythological quivers
coming under humble pie
weeping to float a daffy-duck
muhammad unscripted, naked
before the first imprint of angel-voice-over
virgil of deep-out insight wars that unite
eventually mingle to arise younger

speculative universes cherry-picking newtonian bowler-hats
sailing pushbuttons invisible enlightenment after yawns
chanting whooping-cranes rebirthing breathless vishnu levels
enraptured in holding-pattern
ockham's art
Neither light nor dark amorphic in-betwixt
depending upon humidity's graviton ray-boat
irony super-nova twinkle-twinkle fiddlesticks
haunted by the pork-barrel radio hamlets addicted to wheelies
spin-rad via evolutionary novelty desiring, it's unique
where no tweets frequent l-band roams aggression wigwags
    their lemony hair
over–population dawns on the beaches & veggie ship-shape
    g-lifts from the horizon
embrace your nimbus, ribboning in our wake vibes quiet buzz
    zigzagging muddles undoing your rd lang necktie, throwing
    arabian gestures wardrobe
unlocking vacant hallways releasing personas from their dark
    hooks
remake our macdonald-forest a listening twilight batty-blue
while silent tiptoeing indian sun–tan now underground with
    the hopi golf-swing
some rude out-a-bonds evil duties' alien invading the new
    muse-eraser track-meet
greek fate puppeting us from hyperspace within nowhere
    unknown death
& us is a worry too, if there is completed shape/shifts' aura
    test
osmosis patterns enigma jigsaw-puzzle distil make your unity
    template
reply unevenly metaphors apocalypse to my lamb-crook
    questioning
inquisition's straw-man lit by your feelings (clean as a queen-
    bee)
& this poem's in our liberty-play that upsettingly always
    escaped

Zukeebukee

lean, eeore leaning upon lean-to's celestial real estate wigwam
attempting to quit this dualistic game-show tit-for-tat?
out-dumb unto suma bonium palimpsest membrane
whispering apocalypse dramas italian calico-cat-burglar
dawning out-to-lunch ensconced by sagging vines
gossips quiet carapaces photon tennis-matches
electronic bombarded auras whirled under
foggy raindrop
scrying open-sky
arabian dervish
still-point null
empty of all but identity itself
letters in the scarves of nightfall
only making facemask a human demon-gene
transparent to all verity
accept this kafka bureaucrat
roto-rooters plumbing einsteins
funky trumpa valentine cheekbones
inside misspellings organic labyrinth of desire
increasingly witless feeling
seeking the cover dark
turn under thy ancient grove
in my redolent bruises' twilit eve
purple shadows full of night lampoons

SEAGULL
FLUFFED UP ON LIZARD YARNING NEEDLES
ALOFT THRU TINTED GAZE
ULTRVIOLENT NAVY QUALIA
CHASING D.C. DENNETT BELOW
THIS OVERSEER AWARENESS
HOMEWORK LAMPOST
CURVED LIKE A PRAYER
It's nurseries' halloween
black petals on rosy faces
diabolical venis-morhia hairy radio
every whiteout no longer up-short

star-player being no-more a killer's life-force
unions of cheap democracies' reformed vim
spooky platinum
magic emotions
rare blue
unseen without feeling
kneeling uniforms
about to spring
their jailers
found only in abstract
mystic theories profound & wildly forgotten
archive seashores left alone islands ruthless cornball
peaked bushy obscurity elephantine mask
ganish hidden underneath what's tuckered-out
nippling goosebumbs' achiles
welded to a catcher's mitt
fading & dyeing josephs upon our twin-sister's iron-box
betrayed via a smorgasbord relativity of infinities' cubbyhole
metaphysical nitty-gritty wiring hermeneutics translated to
    echo psyche
coined image reeling question marks
up-standing in the open
like a funny rhinoceros quarterback
globe-trotting with miss everyone
bunny-hopping devil-dust
dodging haywire signs
instantly in front of you
supervening oblivion's amnesia
descartes nega-tiva my zetetic intuition
jiggling this country road's medieval tale
here umbillical bars wink rocket-ships
imbibed electron no-place at once
climb in with dart-board mumbly-peg
winding up this buzz
imagining proust humidity
syncopated, contextual
iterated truth, mendacious
after its general register

chimes only the unique
when nothing is empty
& always fully magnified
you burn synesthesia rainbows
outa-sight, dendrite, tree-house

Yaffle doke prokaryates
gigeriun enthymeme clamjamery
qhit jouk hield stulm ettle zuburb
mayachs yclept ola anthineria luff
one muckling nickaloanian verving thru the sound-barrier
pigtail bangs justice waiting for an iceberg
spinning-in like a big warm grin of halloween
open thumbs intelligence is your act, laughing daffodils
instead of a tombstone epitaph, I've got my ill- fortunes' tone-
    deaf
now we've rubatoed deities masquerade waggling virtue, tap-
    dancing elevator-shoes
all is creation, feel your hum as you bumblebee thy
    underground arising in suez
awareness radiating limbs of weeping-willows caught by the
    breath of the sky

(to gene ruggles)

I'm jiving my fictions
illusions are the mirage I live
every moment seems impossible to co-exist
unless we sleep into dream then all is probable
& I'm alive, yet nothing delays the same flimflam
or at least iterates it's repeat
hiatus jumping categories & states
modes open their dishonest verandas to the starry black
hazy turquoise gleam platinum thin appears up wishing-wells'
    cannon-mouth

like an unlikable funny reflection drowning me in tarnished
   purple-mirrors
cloyed pith helmet opium-sweets, gingering my wilder focus
   vague
to bring on deep shapes lambent legerdemain growing whole
   persons
rhadamantine marly yashmak capriole exheredated gazumping
   derf
keep, leap underneath this art of entertaining numinous real-
   estate jackanapes
pulling up their vampire stakes in a blizzard of myths like a
   drunken rose

solar tweak to enter bone invisible in ivory waters
taking on hues of yous, reflections caught within become fire-
   opals
in my toads eye anti-entropic, gobbledeegok webfooted
   kicking h20
signals from wild organ-grinders blank pluck impulse jargon
intercepting bio-imprints of every kind laws & flood-gates
now I'm in my anti-bio zoot-suit with mayday dental &
a breath of grey machinery, othering worlds as henry miller
   unsaid to y'all
from molar radio, each letter ithunn powers overhead,
   underneath in-between
throughout & deep within the outside now lullaby fipple-flute
   tectonic a jiggle in the vibe-tribe durative title-waves relapse
   be a reed composed by a gust
                              sailing accidental riffs
                     oxygen wagon-trains bonnet
                  life with a life intricately vast
polarities green-grocer nerve-flash communications must now
   reach I, u, it & we as ye engineer howdy-duty & ragiedy-
   anne, lauren bacal & oscar wilde ampersands musical hip-
   hopped-up doing a do-see-do with random flux touring
   easter-bunnies haunted-hunt
experince gives truth if interpreeded via acorresponednt hermit

& a blazing native in celestial flames unstoppable as killing
death.

before once

Reality just disguised surprise
elbows violining incarnated museums zoom
tripping within innumerable-selves
immunology jails open to misallanious alien
suchs leading & grouping
wholeisms outa-duh hemmingway corral
ratiocination fired viva passion's bliss
linked to a wrathful tigerous evergreen
never to be sawed into computer-bits
alive beyond reincarnated novelty
event & event mayaed
here's non-real aftermath
sweeping thou to thou
golden dust in the flame of the air's poof
imaginative elves waiting on startled timelessness
necktied upon a chinese junk
diadems boxing light-heaven

H. D. Moe

CPSIA information can be obtained
at www.ICGtesting.com
Printed in the USA
JSHW022035120323
38849JS00001B/7